potluck at
midnight
farm

potluck at
MIDNIGHT FARM

*Celebrating Food, Family,
and Friends on Martha's Vineyard*

tamara weiss

WITH A FOREWORD BY
carly simon

PHOTOGRAPHS BY
nina bramhall

clarkson potter/publishers
NEW YORK

FOR

Gary, MY SOULMATE, WHO FEEDS ME LOVE EVERY DAY,
AND FOR **Noah** AND **Jules**, MY EVERYTHING

Copyright © 2002 by Tamara Weiss
Photographs copyright © 2002 by Nina Bramhall

All rights reserved. No part of this book may be reproduced or transmitted in any form or by any means, electronic or mechanical, including photocopying, recording, or by any information storage and retrieval system, without permission in writing from the publisher.

Published by Clarkson Potter/Publishers, New York, New York.
Member of the Crown Publishing Group.

Random House, Inc. New York, Toronto, London, Sydney, Auckland
www.randomhouse.com

CLARKSON N. POTTER is a trademark and Potter and colophon are registered trademarks of Random House, Inc.

Printed in Japan

Design by Marysarah Quinn

Library of Congress Cataloging-in-Publication Data
is available upon request.

ISBN 0-609-60909-2

10 9 8 7 6 5 4 3 2 1

FIRST EDITION

contents

foreword

No one minds that tonight's sunset is dunked in a gray-blue mist. Fog comes in from that place where fog waits and it removes the horizon line. The waves rise like a breath and break with almost no notice. Our faces appear just rosy, and no color looks quite like itself. Every tone is muted in this wafty universe, but the sounds of lemonade melting the ice in the glasses and lobster claws being cracked open are sharp and distinct. The potluck dinner is just getting under way.

We are the teenagers. We have removed ourselves from the "child" category.

Our speech is more self-conscious. We have a looking-over-the-shoulder awareness of the approaching night. We're excited to see each other again after the school year. Natasha, Chrissie, Erica, the Benson boys, my sisters and brother, my cousin Jeanie, and me. Our gossip, itching to be told, is both whispery and modulated by organized bursts of laughter. Our eyes scan each other's bodies, quickly, with newly acquired subtlety, but we're definitely checking each other out. Who's wearing which with what? Is there a bathing suit under those Bermuda shorts? Has Joan bleached her hair? (Yikes, that would be really cheeeap!) Is that lipstick or just coral-colored sunblock? Oh, the questions!

Lucy has modestly left her guitar behind in our parent's Chevy in the parking lot at Menemsha Beach. Potentially we know enough chords between us to play at least two songs. Will the demand be strong enough and will it coincide with an optimistic five-minute window of self-confidence? Later. After we eat.

"There's a square dance tomorrow night at the Community Center."

"I'm more interested in the folk sing on Friday. I hear Jessie and Davy are going to be singing."

"Oh God, I love her. She's so beautiful."

"I love him. I want to marry him."

One of the grown-ups passes us beers. We won't remind him who we are and how old we are. Another grown-up starts the bonfire. Beach towels are assembled around the warmth. Someone has set up a slab of wood between two lobster crates to create some organization. What a delightful still life: plastic glasses and beer bottles are parked there. Pitchers of punch, shallow dishes of guacamole surrounded by chips, shrimp on a plate with mayonnaise sauce, tin foil filled with garlic bread, macaroni salad, potato salad, brownies. Each dish a contribution from a different guest. Who's the host? Couldn't possibly tell you. Didn't matter. Still doesn't.

Now that I think back on the menu, it seems so rudimentary. Possibly my unsophisticated palate didn't notice the oregano sprinkled on top of the pieces of garlic bread or the saffron in the rice salad. This book is about noticing the saffron. About the individual touch. The fun and imagination of each contribution.

Potluck derives from the word *potlatch,* which means "to give." This is from a Chinook tradition, which apparently began as a special ceremony for a deceased member of a certain clan. Opposing clan members were invited to attend this raucous event, and hierarchies were established between rival clans based on who could eat the most. What has survived from the original tradition is the fun and the revel. There is always music, often dancing, and there is sometimes rain (and a makeshift relocation). There are inevitably laughing children running barefoot, sandy or muddy, through a kitchen.

Tamara's kitchen is the one I think of. Her and Gary's twins, Jules and Noah, have seen more than a handful of potlucks this past year as we prepared this book, photographing each occasion for the benefit of cooks and readers everywhere. Tamara is a childhood friend of mine. We are as thick as thieves. She got me involved with this book because she gets everyone excited about everything. Potluck is a subject I love. It has a real sense of aesthetic practicality to me. No one has to do all the work. It is shared. It is something to discuss and to take pride in. A community of cooks who have time to enjoy the party because they haven't spent all day over a hot stove. The only major thing to worry about is to remember to take home the plate you came with. Whatever you do, don't get slack and bring Tupperware. Show some style and put your shrimp aspic on your grandmother's best Spode china serving plate!

Carly Simon

introduction

I am an organizer. I am an assembler. I am a table setter. I'm not a cook.

As a child, growing up in New York, I used to volunteer to put away the groceries so that I knew exactly where the black and white cookies from Mother's Bake Shop would be hiding. My job for dinner was to set the table, a task I loved as long as I could choose which napkins went with which place mats all by myself. I put the salads together. I loved to wash the lettuce, cranking the top of the spinner round and round until the leaves were perfectly dry and I was exhausted. I liked to peel and slice the cucumbers, but only after I had carved a few faces in the waxy skin. Best of all, I loved to light the candles.

During the 1960s, both of my parents were active in the antiwar movement. Many important meetings were held at meals around our dining room table, which when opened wide could seat up to fourteen. If there were too many people to sit easily at the table, everyone would move into the living room, taking their plates piled high with them. I would pass the bread, pour the wine, clear the food away, all the while getting a lesson in peace and conflict resolution.

The kitchen was a constant hub of activity. Everyone was allowed to help clean up, but my father ruled where dish washing was concerned.

My mother traveled to Vietnam several times when I was young. My sister, brother, and I always knew when she was going because the cupboards would be overflowing with our favorite foods. My mother liked to feed us. To this day, she likes to feed everyone.

We spent our summers on Martha's Vineyard. I remember the parties at my parents' house well. People arrived by foot either up the long stairs from the beach or through a path in the woods. They came on bicycles or in cars, and they never came empty-handed. They brought homemade bread, bottles of wine, pots of clam chowder, blueberry pie, and bouquets of wildflowers. If we were lucky, someone brought a watermelon just for us kids. My mother made certain there would be enough for everyone. I may not have inherited her culinary skills, but I did learn how to organize an event around food.

Fortunately, years later, I married a cook. I met my husband, Gary, on the Vineyard, dancing at the once-celebrated Hot Tin Roof nightclub. On our first date he made me dinner, and he has cooked for me ever since.

We left downtown Manhattan for up-island Martha's Vineyard, where we decided to live year-round with our two sons. We traded our fourth-floor walk-up for a two-hundred-year-old farmhouse surrounded by stone walls and lilac groves. I opened a home furnishings store with my dear friend Carly Simon; we named it Midnight Farm.

The store is in the port town of Vineyard Haven, and it's become more than a store; it's a place for people to gather. The environment, with its comfortable furniture, candles (always burning), world music, and visual pleasures, is stimulating to the senses, constantly evolving, and ever changing. Old friends run into one another and new friends are easily made. With all the comforts of home, it draws people in and encourages them to linger.

Carly and I have met many wonderful people at Midnight Farm since we opened several years ago. It is from this store that the inspiration for a potluck cookbook was born.

There is a certain lifestyle on the Island, one that mixes locals with summer residents, fishermen with writers, and gardeners with actors. Coming together over food is an obvious way to celebrate our lives here.

We like to eat potluck style on the Vineyard. As a full-time working mother (who refuses to give up her social life), I find potlucks by far the easiest and most enjoyable way to see friends. Everyone contributes so I don't have to spend hours in the kitchen or a week's paycheck at the market. Empty dishes are taken home with departing guests so there's far less clean-up.

The best part, naturally, is the wide selection of homemade food. Guests often make their favorite dishes with the desire to please as many friends as possible. Some potlucks are completely spur of the moment. If Gary should happen to be out fishing and lucky enough to catch a keeper bass, I might get the call at work that sends me into an immediate potluck-organizing mode for that night. He will grill the fish, someone will bring a salad, another a bag of corn, and someone else, maybe, a bowl of berries. After work I come home to set the table and light the candles, and a delicious and spontaneous meal is enjoyed by all.

Once you get into potluck mode you can plan any gathering—Sunday night suppers, birthday parties, even a wedding—as a group effort. Of course, larger events require more planning. The host is usually the one to put together the menu. You start by suggesting a general category for the guests: an appetizer, a salad, main course, dessert. The guests have the option of picking something seasonal, or it may be the theme of the party that inspires them to prepare a dish. I always ask, "What do you *want* to make?" and then decide if that fits with my menu. There are always flowers, wine, bread, or watermelon to be purchased and brought by those guests who don't cook or have the time.

It's important to cover the bases. Try to have something for everyone. If you know certain friends don't drink alcohol, make sure there will be plenty of alternatives like sparkling cider, nonalcoholic beer, or fresh lemonade. Have lots to offer vegetarians, and it's a good idea to serve fresh fruits alongside scrumptious desserts. Children are always welcome at my potlucks (after all, I do have two boys in the house), so I include them when I plan a menu. And I've found that the invited guest who will be bringing a child is a good person to ask to bring something special for the kids.

An abundance of food comes directly from this beautiful island. We can always find fresh fish at the markets (right off the boats in Menemsha), or if we're feeling truly inspired, we grab a bucket and our permit and dig our own clams, mussels, scallops, or oysters. Potluck on this island is certain to include seafood.

Roadside stands and the farmer's market are brimming with gorgeous organic fruits and vegetables. We support our local farmers whenever possible. They work hard to bring us the freshest foods. We can buy milk and cream from Island dairies, local honey, and bottled water from up-island springs. These are options that are available all across the country if you only take the time to search them out. Selecting food when it's this fresh makes preparing it more of a pleasure. Potlucks, where people grab a plate and help themselves, do not require fancy food. They require food that is appealing to look at and that tastes divine. Simple is good.

Food brings people together in so many ways. I often hear people meeting for the first time while oohing and aahing over dishes and platters of homemade food. "What do you suppose that is?" or "Would you like some of this?" usually turns into "My name is so and so" and "Which one of these beautiful dishes is yours?"

It's good to add new faces to your usual circle of friends. I love an intimate gathering but find I come from the school of thought that says the more the merrier. (It's the same school my mother went to, for sure.) Sometimes I get out of control and want my good friends to know my other good friends and I want both of those groups to meet my new friends. I know I'm in trouble when I start inviting people I know to other people's potlucks.

Potlucks are about people and food. We choose to eat this way because it's casual and fun. Music is a key to any successful party, unless you are entertaining outside, listening to the pounding ocean or barnyard orchestra. Live music is always the best; if you have a friend who plays the guitar, banjo, or mandolin, tell him or her to bring it along. Spontaneous outbursts of singing and dancing hardly need encouragement at a successful party.

This past year there were dozens of potlucks on Martha's Vineyard. Some were for book groups, garden clubs, or French clubs, some were for church groups, others were fund-raisers. Some were simply for getting together with people we love to celebrate food, family, and friends.

This book is a sampling of the latter kinds of potlucks. The ones not listed in the calendar section of the local paper. These eleven events were real parties that happened on the Vineyard over the course of a year. Documenting those potlucks with her ever-ready camera in hand was my great friend and neighbor Nina Bramhall. Nina is a freelance photographer who specializes in gardens, portraiture, and lifestyle. Nina moved to the Vineyard with her husband, Paul, and son, Nathaniel (Natty), shortly after we did. Our children have been best friends since birth and many of our potlucks are shared events. Her photographs truly capture our Vineyard potluck style.

Patrie Grace, also a great friend and familiar face on the potluck circuit, has lived on Martha's Vineyard for the past twenty-three years. She owns a successful business called With Grace, coordinating and consulting for weddings and events. She tested each of the following recipes from these eleven parties. Translating them from the original (and often illegible!) handwriting of some of my friends was at times a daunting task. One thing we all agree upon is that the recipes are simple and the outcome delicious.

On the following pages you will see the beautiful island we call home and meet some of the people who live here. I have asked them to write a word or two about their recipe or potluck contribution; in this way you will get to know them better. What you will find is an eclectic group of people who have chosen to live on an island off the tip of Cape Cod. We are a family of fishermen, doctors, teachers, retailers, carpenters, singers, artists, realtors, poets, and chefs. We honor this island and celebrate one another throughout all seasons of the year.

tamara's tips
for hosting a successful potluck

I have potlucks because they are fun. They are delicious. They have the added bonus of being cost-effective and easy on a working mom's schedule. They provide an adventurous and spirited approach to food. But you can't be shy and throw an effective potluck. You need to know what you want and ask for it. You need to delegate jobs to your friends or family, and you need to be organized. What follows is a list of some of the questions I ask myself and the steps I take when I plan a potluck. It's not exhaustive—it can't be, since each party will have special requirements. But it provides a road map.

Where's the party?

Should it be small or large? Indoors or out? In a meadow or on the beach?

Parties can be a lot of fun when they're held in unexpected places. Martha's Vineyard has so many beautiful beaches, trails, and fields with great views. You should look for similar locations and gather your friends there. Be prepared for more planning, though. The first questions to ask are: Is it legal to have a party there? To drive there? To build a fire? Remember that you won't be able to dash into your kitchen for matches, salt, bottle openers, garbage bags, ice—or an extra blanket or sweater or more sunblock—so make an exhaustive list and check everything off as you pack it. Make sure the site is not far from parking (a long walk laden with heavy baskets is the quickest way to dampen your guests' spirits), and also make sure you take out everything you brought in. Cleanup is as essential as setup.

Is there a theme?

You might be planning a casual get-together, but if you've decided on Mexican night, for example, that will set a tone for how you decorate.

Who's coming?

Your guest list is the most important part of a potluck. Invite friends who know one another, but be sure to include some new faces, too. I always want to introduce people to one another. Just because we live on a small island doesn't mean we all know one another. Introduce your guests!

Pick a main course.

This is where you start when you're planning your menu, whether you intend on making the entrée yourself or someone else will provide it. It gives your guests a direction for the dishes they will bring. I think the best menus are based on foods that are fresh and in season.

Call your guests.

Be ready to suggest a category—hors d'oeuvre, salad, side dish, dessert—and don't be afraid of letting your guests know if something doesn't fit with your theme and suggesting an alternative.

Have a list of ideas ready for friends who don't cook. There are a lot of possibilities here, from store-bought brownies or ice cream to watermelon or berries or corn or oysters. But there are also more essentials for a party, like sparkling water, juice, wine, beer, coffee and tea, flowers, candles, firewood—or even extra glasses or dinner plates.

Remind the guests bringing hors d'oeuvre to be on time. (I always provide at least one thing to nibble on, to be on the safe side.)

Ask guests to bring along serving utensils for their dish and to use attractive serving dishes. (No aluminum or plastic, please!)

Let your guests know how many people are attending the potluck. And remember that for large parties, you don't need to ask that each dish serve the full complement of guests.

Check the menu.

This is the time to make sure you've got all the courses covered and that you've allowed for the wants of all your guests. Enough nonalcoholic beverages? Enough for the vegetarians to eat?

Children are often included at potlucks, so it's important to have plenty of food and beverages that will keep them happy. If there will be a lot of kids, provide a baby-sitter; your friends will thank you. I set up a kids' table, and I try to think of activities. For outside parties, I provide balls and bats or Frisbees. Inside, I might have a supply of rubber stamps and markers. And at dessert time, create-your-own ice cream sundaes and cupcake decorating are always a hit. If the children are happy, the parents will be, too.

Plan your setting.

For buffet tables, place dinner plates at one end and knives, forks, and napkins at the other to make it easier for guests to pile their plates high with food. A separate table for beverages and glasses can be a good idea, too. Make sure you have enough plates, glasses, utensils, table linen, and the like.

Arrange for containers for ice and beverages that should be served cold. I often use big galvanized tubs filled with ice.

Flowers are mandatory.

I like flowers on the food table, dining table, kids' table—even in the bathroom. I always have flower arrangements at my outdoor potlucks, too. Old sap buckets or watering cans make great vases.

So are candles.

Candles go so far toward creating a mood for a party. I scatter votives all over the house. Pillar candles are nice on the main dinner table. (I use flat beach stones as bases for the shorter or wider pillars.) For outdoor potlucks, set out lanterns, tiki torches, and citronella candles.

If there are children around, keep candles away from those small hands. And never place scented candles near food.

Music sets the tone.

Choose your CDs ahead of time and have music playing when people arrive.

Have an additional selection of CDs stacked in anticipation of changing moods throughout the night.

Do you have friends who might provide live music? Invite them to bring along their instruments.

Cleanup is fun.

Guests are responsible for their own dishes and utensils, which makes the start of cleanup a breeze.

Make sure you have plenty of garbage bags, plastic wrap, dish soap, and dish towels on hand.

Never say no to offers of help. A potluck is a collective effort, and cleaning up at the end should be a part of the party. Plus, those conversations in the kitchen are always the best.

Relax.

Have fun at your party and embrace the unexpected. Things happen. You're set up outside for a party for fifty. It rains. Move the party inside. Francesca accidentally sits in the frosted fudge brownies that were left on a chair in the kitchen. Lend her a pair of jeans (she might keep them). Danny said he was bringing rice and shows up instead with guacamole. Open a bag of chips. Judy said she was bringing one guest and arrives with four. Relax—there's always enough food.

Don't panic, just go with the flow. Remember that you are hosting the party because you want to spend time with your guests. Celebrate your family, friends, and food! Laugh, sing, dance, and eat.

spring
POTLUCKS

LOVE YOUR
mother's day
BRUNCH

When I was a child, Mother's Day meant giving my mother something I had made with my own small hands. I can still hear her cries of delight at the sight of a clay coil pot, a spatter painting, or a wooden napkin holder (the one I made in shop when I was five sits prominently on her kitchen counter thirty-five years later). In the evening we would sit down to dinner surrounded by grandmothers, grandfathers, and any of my parents' friends who may have been in need of a home-cooked meal. Mom spent an awful lot of time working in the kitchen on Mother's Day.

As I grew older the presents changed from handmade to store-bought: a pair of dangly earrings, a scarf, a book (all purchased with her charge card accompanied by a handwritten note saying I was indeed her daughter and could spend her money!). Now that I have children of my own it's easy to come up with the perfect gift for my mother—a picture of my boys. The delighted cries have turned into a heartfelt sigh and nothing could be more desirable.

Some people think flowers, or breakfast in bed. On the Vineyard, in my family, we think: Gather some friends for brunch at the Whiting Farm! Potluck! Mother's Day! Time to celebrate.

The Whiting Farm sits on what I truly believe must be the exact center of Martha's Vineyard. Before you reach Alley's General Store (on your right going up-island), it's impossible not to notice the big old Victorian, surrounded by numerous barns and outbuildings. Animals have the run of the wild, and on any given day you might see Percy or Lilith, the dogs, Clover, the cow, or Dreamer, the one-eyed horse, roaming the fields. For certain you will see sheep. The Whiting Farm is one of the few remaining island farms, and Allen's family is the eleventh generation to raise sheep.

One might also see Allen's wife, Lynne, a fourth and fifth-grade teacher at the small Menemsha School, riding the lawn mower or tending to her garden. Allen zigzags between his art studio, gallery, and the barn. When not behind the wheel of his tractor, Allen is painting. His landscapes are highly regarded both on and off the island.

Allen and Lynne are the kind of friends who say yes immediately, followed by "What can we make?" at the suggestion of a gathering in their backyard. We dragged out a farm table, found benches and chairs, and set the table for an informal Mother's Day celebration. Friends arrived with children in tow, carrying bagels, scones, yogurt, granola, fruit, salmon, fritattas, and other midmorning delights. With no need for a kitchen we managed to pull off a small feast outside. An animal orchestra replaced Vivaldi. Children played tag, dangled from trees, and chased Percy and Lil. The sweet smell of lilacs filled the air.

Looking down the table I realized we were truly an eclectic group. Assembled together were single mothers, widowed mothers, stepmothers, godmothers, married mothers, and new mothers of adopted children. How could we *not* celebrate? We raised our coffee mugs and toasted the animals, our children, our partners, and the amazing art of mothering.

blue moon granola

WENDY MUELLER BRAUN

You only get granola this *good once in a blue moon!*

MAKES 4 1/2 QUARTS OR 20 CUPS

8 cups rolled oats
2 cups barley flakes
2 cups wheat flakes
2 cups oat bran or wheat germ (or some of each)
2 cups raw sunflower seeds
2 cups pecans, broken or chopped into pieces
1/2 cup oil (canola or safflower)
1/2 cup honey
1/2 cup maple syrup
1 cup dried cranberries
1 cup raisins

Heat the oven to 325 degrees.

Combine the oats, barley flakes, wheat flakes, oat bran, sunflower seeds, and pecans in a large bowl and mix. Stir the oil, honey, and maple syrup in a medium saucepan over low heat until warm. Pour heated mixture over the dry ingredients and mix thoroughly. Spread the granola out in thin layers on large baking sheets and bake for 20 minutes. Stir and bake another 20 minutes. The granola is done when it is golden brown all over.

Use a spatula or large spoon to transfer baked granola to a bowl. Repeat the baking process until all the granola is done. When cool, stir in the cranberries and raisins.

Store in quart-size containers. This granola also freezes well.

NOTE: This is delicious with plain yogurt flavored with maple syrup and a bit of ground cinnamon.

luscious fruit salad

TAMARA WEISS

I could be stranded on a desert island as long as there was plenty of fruit. I can't go a day without it. There isn't a fruit I don't like to eat, and during the peak season, the summer months, I am perfectly content to live as a fruitarian.

Any combinations of fruits will make a fruit salad, as long as you cut and assemble them in an artful manner. Foraging for berries is particularly delightful on a hot summer's day—I have yet to meet anyone who doesn't enjoy gathering the goods.

In the winter months, citrus salads loaded with grapefruit, oranges, clementines, and dried cranberries are sure to keep a cold at bay. If your child begs for a mango for dessert instead of an ice cream sandwich, you know you are doing something right! SERVES 10 TO 12

1 large, ripe honeydew melon
1 large, ripe cantaloupe
2 cups watermelon chunks, seeds removed
1½ pounds seedless grapes, cut in half
2 oranges, peeled, sectioned, and seeded
3 ripe peaches, pitted and cut into bite-size pieces
1 banana, peeled and sliced into ¼-inch rounds
1 pint strawberries, cut in half
1 pint blackberries (leave them whole)
1 pint raspberries (leave them whole)
1 lime
Fresh mint for garnish

Cut the honeydew melon and cantaloupe in half and scoop out the seeds. Slice these halves into wedges, cut off the rinds, then cut the melon into small chunks. Place these in a large glass or ceramic bowl. Toss in the watermelon. Next the grapes, oranges, and peaches. Place the banana rounds on top, but refrain from stirring or the salad will become mushy. Add the strawberries, blackberries, and raspberries to the top of the fruit salad. Squeeze the juice from the lime halves all over the fruits. Garnish with fresh mint leaves, then *gently* toss just before serving. I use my hands for this as they bruise the fruits less than any utensils.

Serve at room temperature or slightly chilled and, if you like, top with raisins, dried cranberries, granola, yogurt, sliced almonds, or rose petals.

bongo scones
blueberry, raspberry, or savory

ROBERT CROPPER

Fresh fruit or savory scones are easily the favorite breakfast item at Bongo, my café on Main Street. True to form, they are loaded with cream and butter. Extravagant, yes. But terribly satisfying. My daughter Olivia and I enjoy making them together, since they are fast, fun, and yummy. Stop by—you may find us engaged in a little pat-a-cake. SERVES 8 TO 12

the scone base
    5 cups all-purpose flour
    2½ teaspoons baking powder
    2½ teaspoons salt
    2½ tablespoons sugar
    1 pound (4 sticks) cold butter, cut into bits
    1⅓ cups heavy cream
    6 large eggs

for blueberry scones
    1½ cups Maine organic frozen blueberries
    Sugar

for raspberry scones
    1 pint fresh raspberries
    Sugar

for savory scones
    ½ pound sharp cheddar cheese, cut into small pieces
    1½ tablespoons finely chopped fresh dill
    Sea salt

Heat the oven to 350 degrees.

Combine the flour, baking powder, salt, and sugar in a large bowl. Cut the butter into the flour with two knives until it resembles coarse cornmeal.

Pour the cream into a different bowl and crack in 5 eggs. Whisk to combine. Add the wet mixture to the dry one. Mix only until combined. Do not overmix.

Divide the dough in half and work with half at a time. Pat it out, then use your fingertips to make holes for filling. Sprinkle on half of the chosen filling and knead lightly and quickly to combine.

Pat the dough into a circle 1 inch thick. Cut into 4 or 6 pieces, depending on the size you like. Place on a baking sheet, leaving 2 inches between scones. Repeat with the other half of the dough.

Beat the last egg with ½ cup water and brush on scones. Sprinkle fruit scones with sugar, savory scones with sea salt.

Bake for 20 minutes.

artichoke heart *and* goat cheese frittata

PATRIE GRACE

Frittatas are a perfect dish to bring to a potluck because they are delicious warm or cold. Leftovers can be eaten for supper with a nice green salad. SERVES 6

1 bunch spring onions or scallions, thinly sliced
2 tablespoons olive oil
1 tablespoon chopped garlic
½ cup basil, finely chopped
1 (14-ounce) can artichoke hearts, drained and quartered
½ cup calamata olives, pitted and sliced in half
¾ cup cherry tomatoes, halved
½ teaspoon sea salt
¼ teaspoon freshly ground black pepper
8 large eggs, well beaten
½ cup crumbled fresh goat cheese

Heat the broiler.

Cook the onions in the olive oil in a large ovenproof skillet over medium heat until the onions are soft and brown, approximately 5 minutes. Add the garlic and cook 1 minute more. Add the basil, artichoke hearts, olives, cherry tomatoes, salt, and pepper. Stir gently, cooking until all vegetables are heated through. Reduce heat to low and pour the beaten eggs on top, covering all the vegetables. Cover and cook until eggs are firm on the bottom, approximately 5 minutes.

Uncover and place under the broiler, watching carefully until frittata is lightly golden. Sprinkle with crumbled goat cheese and return to broiler for 1 minute.

Cut and serve.

cranberry lemonade

LYNNE WHITING

I couldn't imagine a more perfect setting for a Mother's Day brunch than in the midst of Mother Earth's presentation of spring on Whiting Farm. To be surrounded by attentive mother sheep and their newborn lambs, the freshly plowed garden, cherished friends, and those individuals nearest and dearest to me—my family—is pure bliss. What a gift it is to be a mother living on Martha's Vineyard! SERVES 10

3 cups freshly squeezed lemon juice (from about 20 lemons)
2 cups superfine sugar
3 cups water
1½ cups cranberry juice
2 lemons, thinly sliced
1 lime, thinly sliced
1 cup fresh cranberries, optional

Strain the lemon juice and combine it with the sugar in a large serving container. (I like wide-mouthed jars.) Stir until sugar is dissolved. Add the water and cranberry juice and stir again. Add a couple of trays of ice to chill the lemonade well. Then add the lemon and lime slices, and the cranberries, if you care to, and serve.

peach *and* roasted pecan coffee cake

PATRIE GRACE

SERVES 10 TO 12

    1 cup whole wheat pastry flour
    1¼ cups unbleached white flour
    2¼ cups turbinado sugar
    ½ teaspoon salt
    1 cup (2 sticks) plus 2 tablespoons unsalted butter, softened
    1 teaspoon baking powder
    ½ teaspoon baking soda
    ⅔ cup buttermilk
    2 large eggs, lightly beaten
    1½ teaspoons vanilla extract
    2 teaspoons ground cinnamon
    1½ cups chopped pecans, pan roasted (see page 89)
    6 large peaches, peeled, halved, pitted, and thinly sliced

Heat the oven to 350 degrees. Butter and flour a 10-inch springform or Bundt pan.

Whisk the whole wheat flour and 1 cup white flour, 1½ cups sugar, and the salt until blended. Cut 1 cup butter into the flour mixture with a whisk until blended. Stir in the baking powder and baking soda. Add the buttermilk, eggs, vanilla, and ½ teaspoon cinnamon. Whisk vigorously until the batter is smooth and fluffy.

Combine ¾ cup pecans, ½ cup sugar, and 1 teaspoon cinnamon in a bowl.

Spread half the batter into the pan. Arrange approximately three-quarters of the peaches on the batter. Sprinkle with the pecan, sugar, and cinnamon mixture. Carefully and evenly spread the remaining batter on top of the peaches.

Mix together the remaining ¼ cup white flour, ¼ cup sugar, ½ teaspoon cinnamon, 2 tablespoons softened butter, and ¾ cup pecans in a small bowl until the mixture is crumbly. Sprinkle over the top of the coffee cake batter.

Bake on the middle rack in the center of the oven for 40 to 45 minutes, until a cake tester or toothpick comes out clean. Transfer the cake to a rack, let cool, then remove pan sides. When completely cooled, slide the cake off the pan bottom onto a serving plate. Surround with the remaining peaches, and garnish the cake with a beautiful rose in the center.

CARLOTTA'S
tea

Carly "Tea" Simon. It should be her middle name. Queen of Tea. Tea fairy. Tea pusher. Rarely have I heard her extend an invitation to Hidden Star Hill, her home in the woods, without suggesting that the visitor would be participating in the sipping of tea.

"We got a new dog. Come for tea."

"There's a crescent moon out. Come for tea."

"I finished a new song. Come for tea."

"Sally's home. Come for tea."

"The willow blew down. Come for tea."

"There's a rainbow over the field. Come for tea."

"Misha was born! Come for tea."

It's the most loving command ever ordered, and anyone who has heard it knows exactly what is in store. Tea at Carly's means conversation—in an overstuffed down chair (the kind one can never get out of), on a pillow on the floor of the screened-in porch, walking through the woods (her dog, Mol, jumping at your heels), or hidden up in the tower, watching the sun disappear into the forest.

No matter where you are, you are certain to be cradling a rather gigantic mug, a bowl really. The larger the vessel, the longer the visit. It takes two hands to drink tea at Carly's, a conspiracy on her part to make you slow down, allowing the tea to relax and comfort you.

Entering Carly's kitchen means ducking if you are over five feet tall. Baskets of all shapes, colors, and sizes dangle from the ceiling, overflowing with boxes and bags of tea. Jars of honey line the shelves. Armed with the necessary fixings, she is always ready for action.

"The peonies are out. Full bloom. Come for tea." The command came in early June, and with it the suggestion to bring a dish for a potluck tea party in her circular garden. Six women were invited and with them came various platters of tea party fare. We kicked off our shoes, entered the garden barefoot, and sat down at a small iron table surrounded by flowers and herbs, the smell of fresh mint, thyme, and lavender in the air.

Carlotta (as some of us call her) provided the tea. We discussed what one talks about when in the company of women and decided that if men drank more tea and planted more peonies, there would be far less war in the world. We sipped our last sip and headed home, bathed in the violet evening light.

the garden tea party

CARLY SIMON

Ah, tea. Tea. So many associations. It is the perfect choice for an afternoon social event. Tea is civility at its least threatening. Tea is age-old. Tea is nice at the magic hour, in a garden, at my house, in June. I have a circular garden. The inner circle is planted with herbs: rosemary, lemongrass, mint, thyme, basil.

Mornings by myself, at 6:00, I take a teapot out to my table in the center of the garden and watch the sun rise. By teatime, it's over the house on the other side of the trees. It passes between the leaves and diffuses through the clouds, which in turn stream a soft pinkish hue on the shrubs, grasses, and flowers in the garden.

I invited a group of women to a potluck tea in June. The offerings from the six guests were largely cakes, puddings, cookies, and sandwiches, but the tea was the named reason for the party, the center of attention you pay no attention to, like a beautiful guest at a party who says very little to anyone, but you can't take your eyes off her.

To make a good tea, there has to be an infusion process. You must let the leaf open and brew in the hottest of water. All you will need for the tea itself are:

A leaf (let's decide on mint for this recipe)—10 to 20 of them
Two teapots (pot #1 and pot #2)
Boiling water
Honey (orange blossom and tupelo are two that go well with all sorts of leaves)

DO IT LIKE THIS: Put the mint leaves into pot #1 and add no more than 1 cup of boiling water. It's always best if the pot wherein you brew is hot. You can achieve this by running it under very hot water from the tap or, better yet, fill it for a bit with boiling water and then empty it just before you add the leaves and the boiling water.

Infuse for 5 to 10 minutes.

Add enough water (from pot #2 or from the kettle on the stove) to fill pot #1.

It can be helpful to add the honey (1 teaspoon per cup) to the water before you take the pots to the garden, or wherever you're pouring the tea. I like my guests to be able to keep their dainty little fingers honey-free. And, without knowing I've already added the honey, all they say is "Oh, it's so sweet," and they seem very happy.

selected teas

Start with 6 cups of fresh, cold water in a kettle. Put 1 teaspoon of loose tea per cup in your ceramic teapot. Pour boiling water on top and let it steep 3 to 5 minutes. Strain through a metal or bamboo strainer by the cup.

for apple ginger tea
¾ cup ginger syrup (recipe follows)
6 cups apple tea (Celestial Seasonings)
6 cinnamon sticks
6 pieces crystallized ginger

Place 2 tablespoons syrup in each of 6 teacups. Fill the teacups with brewed apple tea, then garnish with cinnamon sticks and crystallized ginger. Serve immediately.

for ginger syrup
1 cup sugar
1 (3-inch) piece fresh ginger

Bring the sugar, ginger, and 1 cup water to boil in a small saucepan. Cool completely (about 1 hour) and strain. Store in an airtight container in the refrigerator for up to 1 week.

for ceylon mint tea
6 tablespoons Ceylon tea
1 bunch (about ½ cup) freshly picked garden mint

Brew the Ceylon tea, adding the mint leaves after 3 minutes of steeping. Pour into teacups and serve with elderflower honey or milk and cream.
   Garnish with a crystallized mint leaf (see page 218), if you like.

artichoke *and* chèvre mousse *on* whole wheat garlic toast

GARY STUBER
brought by tamara weiss

There are several advantages to having a husband who cooks. One of them is getting him to prepare a most elegant, delicious, and totally original creation. The disadvantage is when you take it to a tea party for women and everyone asks you for the recipe. Well, here it is. SERVES 10

4 fresh artichokes
6 shallots, minced
8 tablespoons olive oil
3 ounces chèvre (fresh goat cheese)
½ cup white wine
Grated zest and juice of 1 lime
¼ teaspoon sea salt
¼ teaspoon freshly ground black pepper
1 package unflavored instant gelatin
2 cloves garlic, peeled and minced
1 whole wheat baguette
Alfalfa sprouts or nasturtium blossoms, for garnish

To prepare the artichokes, cut off the tips and cut back the stems. Place them, stems down, in a large stockpot in 2 inches of water. Cover and boil over medium heat until a knife passes through the center easily (25 to 30 minutes). Check water level often to make sure it hasn't boiled away. Drain and when cooled, remove the outer leaves. You will have what looks like a thistle flower. Cut around the base of the thistle and remove it with a paring knife. Quarter the heart with stem and set aside.

Sauté the shallots in 2 tablespoons olive oil until tender.

Put the artichoke hearts, shallots, chèvre, wine, lime zest and juice, salt, and pepper in a blender. Blend until liquefied. Pour this mixture into a medium saucepan. Heat on medium but do not boil.

Whisk in the gelatin. Remove from heat. Pour into a mold of your choice. Refrigerate until set (1 to 2 hours).

Place the garlic and 6 tablespoons olive oil in a blender. Puree. Warm this mixture in a small saucepan over low heat. Slice the baguette thinly and lightly toast under the broiler or in a toaster oven. Brush the toasts with garlic oil.

Unmold the mousse by turning it upside down on a board and tapping the bottom. If it sticks, run a butter knife around the edges. Cut the mousse into approximately ¼-inch slices, place on toasts, and serve. (Maintain the light texture of the mousse by not spreading it.) Garnish with alfalfa sprouts or nasturtiums.

roasted red pepper
roll-ups

PATRIE GRACE

MAKES 20

1 red bell pepper, halved and seeded
½ cup fresh mint, washed and chopped
4 (8-inch) flour tortillas
½ cup chèvre (fresh goat cheese)
Salt and freshly ground black pepper

Heat the broiler.

Broil the pepper, skin side up, for 5 to 10 minutes, until charred. Place in a small bowl with a plate on top to cool completely. Uncover and peel off the skin.

Chop finely. Combine the mint and chopped pepper in a bowl.

Heat a frying pan over medium heat. Cook tortillas one at a time until warm, about 15 seconds. Flip and do the same on the other side. Remove to a plate and cover with a towel. Repeat with the remaining tortillas.

Spread each tortilla (one at a time) with about 2 tablespoons of the goat cheese and one-fourth of the mint and chopped pepper mixture. Sprinkle with salt and pepper. Roll up the tortilla firmly. Wrap the rolled tortilla in plastic wrap, twisting the ends of the wrap to secure. Repeat with the other 3 tortillas. Refrigerate for 1 hour.

Remove the tortillas from the refrigerator and cut each tortilla diagonally into 5 slices. Serve at room temperature.

honey's
cherry tomato kabobs

PATRIE GRACE

MAKES 16

1 yellow bell pepper, halved and seeded
1 clove garlic, finely chopped
2 tablespoons olive oil
1 tablespoon fresh lemon juice
16 baby mozzarella balls
Sea salt and freshly ground black pepper
1 bunch (about 1 cup) fresh basil leaves, finely chopped, plus 16 large fresh basil
   leaves
1 pint large cherry tomatoes, halved
16 thin metal or wooden skewers

Heat the broiler.

Broil the pepper, skin side up, for 5 to 10 minutes, until charred. Place in a small bowl with a plate on top to cool completely. Uncover and peel off the skin. Chop finely.

Mix the pepper, garlic, oil, lemon juice, mozzarella, $\frac{1}{2}$ teaspoon sea salt, and $\frac{1}{2}$ teaspoon pepper. Let stand for 30 to 40 minutes to marinate. Toss in the chopped basil.

Thread your skewers, keeping the ingredients toward the beginning of the skewer, first with a cherry tomato half, next the marinated mozzarella, then the other tomato half, wrapped in a basil leaf, at the tip. Serve at room temperature.

lambert's cove lemon tea cake

CINDY DOYLE

This cake is good anytime—from breakfast to midnight snack. It will also keep well, but that depends on one's ability to resist temptation. In our house we have perfected the art of "shaving," and if you want to learn how to shave, this is the perfect cake to practice on. Shaving begins at the dinner table after your first piece of cake is finished. Everyone sits around the table talking about how delicious the cake was, saying they're too full for a second piece. After a few minutes someone sitting strategically near the cake picks up the knife and announces that he or she is just going to have a sliver. Another person nearby notices the person who cut the sliver left an uneven edge and offers to help even it off. And so it goes around the table, each person shaving, slivering, and evening. If there's any cake left, shaving can continue at the kitchen counter at midnight (which saves on dirty dishes) or the next day eating straight out of the refrigerator with the door open (refreshing on a hot summer day). Note: There is one rule of shaving etiquette—the person who finishes the cake washes the dish. SERVES 10 TO 12

the cake
    2 large lemons, zest grated finely
    1 tablespoon finely grated orange zest
    3 tablespoons fresh lemon juice
    1 tablespoon fresh orange juice
    3 cups sifted all-purpose flour
    ½ teaspoon baking soda
    ½ teaspoon salt
    1 cup (2 sticks) unsalted butter, softened
    3 cups granulated sugar
    5 extra-large eggs
    1 cup buttermilk

the glaze
    ¼ cup fresh lemon juice
    1 tablespoon fresh orange juice
    ½ cup granulated sugar

    Confectioners' sugar

Adjust the oven rack in the bottom third of the oven and heat the oven to 325 degrees. Butter a 10-inch tube pan and line the bottom with waxed paper; butter the paper.

To make the cake, mix the lemon and orange zests with the lemon and orange juices in a small bowl and set aside. Sift together the flour, baking soda, and salt in a separate mixing bowl and set aside.

Cream the butter with an electric mixer in a large mixing bowl. Gradually add the sugar and beat at medium-high speed for 2 to 3 minutes, until light. Add the eggs one at a time, beating after each addition until they are fully incorporated. Beat for an additional 2 to 3 minutes after the last egg has been added. On the lowest speed add the sifted dry ingredients in small amounts, alternating with the buttermilk in a slow stream, scraping the bowl with a rubber spatula and beating just until smooth after each addition. Stir in the lemon and orange zests and juices by hand. Scrape the batter into the pan. Rotate the pan briskly back and forth several times to level the batter. Bake 1½ hours, or until a cake tester comes out dry.

Make the glaze as soon as the cake is put into the oven. Mix the juices, granulated sugar, and 1 tablespoon water and let stand, stirring occasionally, while the cake is baking.

When the cake is done, remove it from the oven and let cool in the pan for 5 minutes. Run a knife around the sides of the pan to loosen the cake. Cover a large plate with a piece of waxed paper. Put the plate with the waxed paper upside down over the cake pan and invert the pan, dropping the cake onto the plate. Remove the pan and leave the cake upside down.

Brush the glaze all over the hot cake with a pastry brush, continuing until all the glaze is absorbed. Let stand until cool and dry.

Sprinkle the cake generously with confectioners' sugar through a fine strainer. Carefully lift the cake off the waxed paper and onto a serving platter.

casey's alaska cookies

EDIE VONNEGUT

At the end of day, when I can't paint anymore, I love to cook. I find it a relief, deeply creative and satisfying to tackle new recipes. There are two things I have zero interest in, microwave ovens and anything that takes time away from the act of assembling a meal. The longer it takes the better I like it. Six-day cassoulets, 12-hour roasts, eternally simmering soups—I love anything that fills the home with good smells.

A prime goal in my life is to have a carefully packed picnic basket ready at all times, with all the essentials, to be able to go from zero to one hundred in getting a picnic under way in the event the weather and tides and friends hit an unexpected perfect pitch. It has to be ever-ready, like a fire extinguisher, only needing some fresh produce plopped in at the last moment. I've almost succeeded, but not quite. Last time I left out a spatula. We ended up using a shingle. MAKES 3 DOZEN

2 cups all-purpose flour
2 teaspoons baking powder
$\frac{1}{4}$ teaspoon salt
2 tablespoons ground cinnamon
2 tablespoons ground ginger
1 cup (2 sticks) unsalted butter, softened
1 large egg
1 teaspoon vanilla extract
3 tablespoons cream cheese
$\frac{1}{3}$ cup molasses
1 (8-ounce) package butterscotch chips
3 Skor candy bars, coarsely chopped
$\frac{1}{3}$ cup coarsely chopped pecans
$\frac{1}{3}$ cup coarsely chopped walnuts
$\frac{1}{2}$ cup sugar

Heat the oven to 350 degrees. Butter a baking sheet.

Sift together the flour, baking powder, salt, cinnamon, and ginger into a mixing bowl.

Cream together the butter, egg, vanilla, cream cheese, and molasses in a second, larger mixing bowl.

Mix the flour mixture, a little at a time, into the butter mixture. Add the chips, chopped candy bars, pecans, and walnuts. Form into small balls, about the size of a golf ball. Pour the sugar into a low bowl and roll each ball in the sugar. Place each ball on a greased baking sheet and bake for 15 minutes. Remove from oven when puffed for chewy cookies or bake 5 minutes more for crispier cookies.

georgia peaches *with* raspberry sauce

JUDITH BELUSHI "GEORGIA" PISANO

I was born in a little cabin in rural Georgia, the oldest of seven kids. Although there wasn't much money for clothes or toys, or even meat (much less books, skates, art supplies, a television, sports equipment, a real bed, or furniture in general), Mama always found time to let each one of us know how special we were. We were her "little Georgia peaches," and Mama loved peaches.

Fact is, we had ten peach trees. If we weren't tending and picking those trees, we were conjuring up recipes for their treasured fruit. Besides the traditional fare, we pickled, deviled, and blackened them, made peach gnocchi, croquettes, pâté, and moonshine to boot. Mama was especially proud of her eleven variations on the aspic salad theme.

Recollections of days past have made me realize that although Mama could not give us much in the way of material goods, the real goods were in the love she instilled in us all for peaches. I gladly share this Georgia peach of a recipe, which, by the way, is also a powerful aphrodisiac. SERVES 12

the peaches and filling
2½ tablespoons unsalted butter, at room temperature
¼ cup brown sugar, packed
1 large egg, beaten
¼ cup finely chopped almonds
2 teaspoons pumpkin pie spice
6 ripe peaches

the sauce
1½ cups fresh raspberries
1 tablespoon confectioners' sugar
1½ tablespoons Chambord liquor

Mint, for garnish

Heat the oven to 350 degrees.

To make the filling, beat the butter and sugar together until smooth. Add the egg to the sugar mixture. Stir in the chopped almonds and spice and set aside.

Halve and pit the peaches. Use a spoon to scrape out some peach around the pit hole to make a nice hollow for the filling. Place the peach halves in a muffin tin (this holds the peach upright) and spoon the filling into the peach hollows. Bake for 30 minutes. The filling top should be lightly browned and the peach tender. Remove from the oven to cool.

To make the sauce, set aside 12 of the prettiest raspberries. While the peaches are cooking mix the remainder of the raspberries, confectioners' sugar, and Chambord in a food processor or blender until smooth. The mixture will still contain seeds and some fiber. Push the puree through a strainer. Chill the sauce while the peaches cool.

Once the peaches are cool enough to handle, gently run a spoon underneath to sever any bonding they've made with the tin. If you want to serve them chilled, you can cover and store in the tin until you are ready to serve. If you wish to serve them warm, place each one on a plate or arrange them together on a platter and spoon the sauce over each peach, making sure to allow some sauce to absorb into the filling. Dribble some decoratively on the plate itself. Garnish with mint and your "perfect" berries and you'll have one good-looking peach sensation. And remember what Mama always said: "Be careful who you share your peaches with. Might could be they'll be back for more."

caramel pecan squares

VICKI GOHL

My Christmas cookie baking partner and I have been making these for ten years, and they are a feature of our annual bake-off. These chewy and beautiful cookies are great with fruit, sorbet, or vanilla ice cream. I often bring them to gatherings and they never fail. These bars will cut small, so you can get 80 cookies from one batch. The recipe doubles beautifully as well. These cookies will keep in the refrigerator for three weeks. MAKES 80 COOKIES

1½ cups (3 sticks) unsalted butter, softened
⅔ cup granulated sugar
2 large eggs, beaten
1 tablespoon vanilla extract
3 cups all-purpose flour
¾ teaspoon salt
⅓ cup maple syrup
⅔ cup brown sugar (light or dark; dark makes darker caramel), packed
2 tablespoons heavy cream
1 generous cup pecans, roughly chopped

Heat the oven to 350 degrees.

Cream together 1 cup butter, the sugar, and eggs until light and fluffy. Add the vanilla, flour, and salt. Press into an ungreased 11×17-inch jellyroll pan. It's a good idea to build the dough up a bit at the edges. Prick with a fork. Bake for 15 minutes; do not brown.

Put the maple syrup, brown sugar, heavy cream, and remaining ½ cup butter in a medium pan and cook over low heat, stirring constantly, until everything melts and combines. Remove from the heat and add the pecans. Spread over the partially baked dough and return to the oven for 25 to 30 minutes, until the topping is caramelized.

Cool on a rack for about 10 minutes, then cut into 80 pieces and remove them from the pan. Place on a rack until completely cooled. I like cutting these on the diagonal for presentation.

summer
POTLUCKS

BLUE
hydrangea

Every summer around mid-July the hydrangeas wrap themselves around Fair Oaks Farm like a band of blue satin around a present. I love these plants. They require very little maintenance and make me feel like I am living in one of those antique hand-colored postcards from Maine. We even have a tiny white picket fence—well, more of a gate—wedged in between two stone walls.

This year, to celebrate the arrival of the various shades of blue blossoms, we decided to have an outdoor potluck dinner. Gary said he would grill some bass, and with the main course agreed upon, I set out to organize the potluck.

Most summer fare goes nicely with fish, so I suggested to people that they bring what they love to make. I made certain all the courses were covered and that those who might be coming straight from work (or who could not cook) would bring watermelon, ice cream, bread, or wine.

Initially, I invited about twelve people and their children (who are always welcome here), but the numbers grew as I went to work each day and greeted more and more friends as they passed through Midnight Farm. The twelve turned into twenty, which turned into thirty, plus kids and houseguests, who brought the number of invited friends to something shy of fifty.

The day of the potluck arrived, and what a glorious day it was. After weeks of rain in July we were finally blessed with blue sky and warm weather. Gary grabbed his waders and fishing rod, shouted "wish me luck!" and headed for the sea. Tables and chairs were borrowed from just about everywhere and the outdoor setup began.

With the help of my friend Patrie, I hung Moroccan lanterns from the branches of the old oak trees. Vintage Mexican tablecloths, weathered

buoys, assorted antique pitchers, watering cans, and vases covered the tables. The flowers were abundant: delphiniums, lilies, roses, and larkspur, all gathered from a friend's garden.

We dragged our old ten-foot farm table outside and set it up as the serving table with plates stacked high on one end, leaving ample room to receive everyone's offerings. A stand for drinks and glasses was arranged next to the hors d'oeuvre table with an old metal washtub from England on the grass below, a perfect vessel for ice.

Various sizes of candles went everywhere, with quahog shells and flat beach stones for bases. Pretty stunning, we thought, as we noticed the hour approaching. Guests were invited for six thirtyish (which means seven in Island time).

"What was that?" I asked Patrie as I stopped dead in my tracks en route inside to change out of my overalls.

"What?" she asked in a panicked tone, as if she imagined me stepping on a dead rabbit with my bare feet.

"That drop, that moisture, that piece of rain I just felt on the back of my neck!" I secretly prayed for a low-flying seagull, but it immediately became apparent that the only low thing in the big blue sky was a dark cloud, and it was hovering over Fair Oaks Farm.

To further remove any doubt, we turned our palms up and frantically paced back and forth across the front yard, attempting to have a calm conversation but realizing that we were screaming.

"*No! It can't be!* This isn't rain, it's only fog!"

"It will stop. Shhh . . . just be quiet."

"*Quiet!* Quiet won't make the rain stop. Oh my God. It's really raining."

"*Okay.* What should we do?"

"*I don't know!* Where's Gary anyway? I can't believe he's still fishing! Okay. What do we do? The plates are getting wet. The napkins are getting wet. It's raining on the hors d'oeuvre table. The olives are getting wet! People are arriving in ten minutes!"

At this point, Noah and Jules were getting an enormous amount of pleasure from watching their mama flip out, running around in circles on the grass. We started to haul everything inside. By this time we were laughing.

Gary arrived somewhere in the middle of the chaos with a huge Larsen's Fish Market bag clutched in his hand. "No keepers," he mumbled, looking slightly dejected as he prepared to light the grill.

A beautiful setup outside does not translate well when it is frantically thrown back inside. Somehow we pulled it off, and instead of mingling under the stars we were ready to hunker down in front of a summer fire.

Yes, it rained, as it had every other day that July. Friends arrived carrying bowls of greens, platters of brownies, baskets of corn, pitchers of margaritas, and bundles of firewood. At one point, the rain stopped and we almost moved everything back outside. It wound up being a slightly indoor, slightly outdoor summer potluck dinner. The blue hydrangeas, soaking up the rain, were perhaps the best nourished of all.

hors d'oeuvre table
if you are not a cook
you can do this!

TAMARA WEISS

If you're not a brilliant cook but have something of an eye, you can always prepare an hors d'oeuvre table. Each day at work I display products, rearrange merchandise, dress mannequins, and create individual environments for the store. Those skills come in handy.

First, you need a small table, preferably one with character or color. Then you need to climb into the way-back of your kitchen cabinets and pull out assorted bowls, plates, cutting boards, vases, buckets, and other treasures you have forgotten existed.

Start with the flowers and create an arrangement with height. Fill the bowls with your various appetizers. Use baskets for crackers, a glass jar for breadsticks, cutting boards or a marble slab for cheeses. Think of fruits—champagne grapes, strawberries, kiwis, and cherries—as the icing on the cake. Drape and arrange them around everything else. Decorate with old wooden fish decoys, large beach stones, or any other interesting objects that catch your eye en route to the table. Remember, this is your opportunity to create. Think Thomas Hart Benton paintings of long, windy roads, and have fun.

the cheeses (large hunks of each)
  Brin d'Amour
  Taleggio
  Huntsman
  Saint André
  Tuscan sheep's milk
  Reblochon
  Morbier
  2 pints fresh mozzarella balls

the olives (¹/₄ pound of each)
  Picholine (small black)
  Greek
  Gaeta
  Cracked green Niçoise

  3 pounds seedless green and red grapes
  1 pound champagne grapes
  6 kiwi fruits
  2 pints strawberries
  1 pint yellow pear tomatoes
  1¼ pounds Jensal Valley
      green and red sun-dried
      tomatoes
  1 (2-ounce) jar Fondodi
      Toscana marinated
      artichoke hearts
  Parmesan breadsticks
  Assorted crackers (I love
      Lavash or Carr's Black
      Pepper crackers)

the vineyard tiler
almost a cranberry margarita

AL STYRON

My fiancé, Ed, and I experimented with drinks when we were tiling the floor of our converted garage one warm July afternoon. Hence the drink's name. It's almost a margarita, but it has no triple sec. As long as the cranberry juice is sweetened, no other sugar is necessary.

Cranberries are indigenous to the Cape and the Islands, which gives our cocktail its special local flavor. The mason jars just make you want to drop your towel and sit down on the porch while the sun disappears into the sea.

MAKES 2 GOOD-SIZE DRINKS

8 ounces high-quality tequila
4 ounces fresh lime juice
4 ounces sweetened cranberry juice
Ice
Margarita salt
Cut limes
½ cup cranberries

Put the tequila, lime juice, and cranberry juice in a large pitcher and stir vigorously. Add lots of ice and stir again.

Pour margarita salt onto a plate. Moisten rims of mason jars with lime, turn upside down, and dip into salt.

Fill the jars and garnish with slices of lime and cranberries.

suff-soóf

tabouli

TONY SHALHOUB

There is as much controversy and debate surrounding this recipe as there is for some presidential elections I know of. Some purists omit the cinnamon; some "whiter" folks like to add cukes or green peppers. Small wars have been fought over just how much lemon juice to use. Feel free to improvise.

The best part of this dish is in the preparation. It's good to get four or five people to help with all the chopping—it's labor intensive. But once the fixings are decided, the group effort brings everyone together and truly adds to the flavor of the dish.

Enjoy! Or, as we say in Arabic, Suk-tyne! SERVES 8 TO 10

1 cup dry bulgur (medium-fine)
2 bunches parsley, finely chopped (no big stems)
1 bunch scallions, finely chopped
1 bunch fresh mint, finely chopped (no stems)
1 tablespoon dried mint, crumbled
1 tablespoon ground cinnamon
2 large tomatoes, finely chopped
$\frac{1}{2}$ cup olive oil
$\frac{1}{2}$ cup fresh lemon juice
$\frac{1}{2}$ teaspoon salt
$\frac{1}{4}$ teaspoon freshly ground black pepper
1 head romaine, for serving
Triangles of pita bread, for serving

Cover the bulgur with 2 cups of cold water and let sit approximately 30 minutes. In the meantime, combine the parsley, scallions, mint (fresh and dried), cinnamon, and tomatoes in a large bowl.

When the bulgur is soft, use your hands to squeeze out the excess water. Add the bulgur to the other ingredients.

Just before serving add the oil, lemon juice, salt, and pepper. Toss and taste for salt and pepper.

Line a serving bowl with romaine leaves and mound in the suff-soóf. Serve with a basket of pita.

cold way hot soba
cold buckwheat soba with hot peanut sauce and tofu

GARY STUBER

In the midseventies I experimented in all directions with organic and natural foods. I began to extrapolate tastes and sensibilities from far-flung cultures. I regularly experimented on my friends, and they must have liked it—they kept coming back for more. Heavy demand to feed neighbors resulted in my opening a small vegetarian restaurant in the Berkshires. The following soba recipe came out of that experience. It was a favorite on the menu then and has withstood the test of numerous potlucks long after I closed the restaurant doors.

The recipe makes more than you'll need for this amount of noodles, but it will keep in the refrigerator for 3 to 5 days. You can find all these ingredients in a good organic food shop. SERVES 8 TO 12

1 pound organic chunky peanut butter
½ cup organic tahini paste
1 quart orange juice with pulp
4 tablespoons curry powder
4 tablespoons tamari sauce
2 tablespoons nori flakes
6 cloves garlic, minced
4 tablespoons French Bonnet red pepper sauce (I like a hot sauce with tamarind)
1½ pounds buckwheat pasta (3 packages)
1 pound organic extra-firm tofu, cubed
¾ cup finely chopped cilantro
½ cup finely chopped scallions
¼ teaspoon cayenne pepper

Combine the peanut butter and tahini in a large saucepan over medium-low heat. Slowly whisk in the orange juice. Add the curry, tamari, nori, garlic, and red pepper sauce. Simmer gently for 10 minutes, whisking often. Do not let it boil. Cool and refrigerate.

Bring a large pot of salted water to a boil and cook the buckwheat pasta until al dente. Drain and rinse in cold water. Drain well. Place the cooled noodles in a large bowl. Top the soba with the cubed tofu, cilantro, and scallions. Pour one-third of the peanut sauce over all and dust with the cayenne.

Toss before serving. Add more sauce as needed.

roasted beets *and* arugula *with* orange zest

JACI PEPPER

SERVES 4 TO 6

8 to 10 medium beets
½ cup olive oil
¼ cup balsamic vinegar
1 tablespoon Dijon mustard
2 cloves garlic, finely chopped
1 tablespoon finely chopped fresh tarragon
2 tablespoons fresh lemon juice
½ teaspoon sea salt
¼ teaspoon freshly ground black pepper
2 bunches arugula
4 ounces chèvre (fresh goat cheese; optional)
4 tablespoons grated orange zest

Heat the oven to 400 degrees.

Wash and trim the beets. Place them on a baking sheet and roast until tender, about 45 minutes. Let the beets cool. When they're cool to the touch, quarter them. You can peel them or not.

Whisk together the olive oil, balsamic vinegar, Dijon mustard, garlic, tarragon, lemon juice, salt, and pepper in a medium bowl.

Wash and dry the arugula and arrange it in a salad bowl. Cover the arugula with beets and pour dressing over the beets. If you are adding goat cheese, crumble it over the beets now. Garnish with grated orange zest and serve.

corn spoon pudding

MARY STEENBURGEN

This is a recipe I grew up with in Arkansas. It is an absolutely guaranteed smash hit. I've made it for all kinds of people who take one bite and instantly want the recipe. It's a little embarrassing to hand it over, since it reads: Open a box of this and a can of that. But trust me, it's the best cornbread you'll ever have.

SERVES 12

1 (8½-ounce) box corn muffin mix
1 (7½-ounce) can whole kernel corn
1 (7½-ounce) can creamed corn
1 cup sour cream
2 large eggs, beaten
½ cup melted unsalted butter
½ cup grated Swiss cheese

Heat the oven to 350 degrees.

Combine all the ingredients except the cheese in a large mixing bowl. Pour into a lightly greased 9×13-inch baking dish. Bake for 35 minutes.

Sprinkle grated Swiss on top and bake 10 minutes more. You will know it's done when a toothpick comes out clean.

Serve warm.

grilled corn guacamole

PAUL SCHNEIDER

I should say up front that everything I know how to make well I learned from my wife, though of course I now secretly believe I make them all much better than she does. But that's just the nature of being male, I suppose. Or, in potential fairness to some males I have not yet met, I guess I should only say it's the nature of being me!

At any rate, if you want to make my wife's already excellent guacamole better than she does, this is how you do it. The corn I use is grilled. Whenever I grill corn, which is whenever I grill anything, which is as often as possible in the summer, I always grill a couple of extra ears. SERVES 10 TO 12

2 ears of corn
6 ripe Hass avocados
2 vine-ripened tomatoes, finely chopped
1 bunch cilantro, chopped
2 limes
¼ teaspoon sea salt
¼ teaspoon freshly ground black pepper
Blue corn chips, for serving

To grill the corn, strip off the outer husks and soak the ears in a little salty water. Roll the ears around on the hot grill until the kernels start to caramelize, approximately 5 minutes per side. Cut the kernels off the cob.

Choose a bowl large enough for mashing and mixing. Cut the avocados in half lengthwise, remove the pit, and scoop out avocado into the bowl. Mash the avocado with a fork until it is lump-free and pretty smooth. Save a tablespoon each of the chopped tomatoes and chopped cilantro for garnish. Add the rest to the avocado.

Squeeze in lime juice and add salt and pepper and grilled corn kernels. Mix it up with your fork.

Garnish and serve with chips.

island blue crab marinara

DIANE ENGLISH

When I was a kid growing up in Buffalo, New York, my family would make the occasional summer voyage to the Jersey Shore for a family reunion. The Italian side of the family was all from South Philly and that was a good meeting spot. We'd rent a small cottage and we'd all cram into the tiny space for a fun week with aunts, uncles, and a thousand cousins. One of my best memories was watching the men haul buckets of blue crabs up to the porch while the women worked all day on the marinara sauce and linguine that was just amazing—even for an eight-year-old.

Recently blue crabs were so plentiful in Vineyard ponds the shellfish constable declared that we could take fifty a person without a license. I decided to try my hand at the crab sauce. After a day of crabbing with my neighbors, we hauled in about twenty good plump ones. They died a glorious death in the marinara sauce, and we are still talking about the fabulous meal. SERVES 8 TO 10

¼ cup olive oil
2 large yellow onions, finely chopped
4 cloves garlic, minced
1 (24-ounce) can tomato puree
1 (24-ounce) can crushed tomatoes
2 teaspoons dried oregano
1 bunch fresh basil, chopped
1 teaspoon salt
½ teaspoon freshly ground black pepper
1 cup Merlot wine
8 to 10 blue claw crabs, rinsed

2 pounds linguine, cooked al dente

Coat the bottom of a large, heavy pot with the olive oil. Add the onions and garlic and cook over medium heat until translucent. Pour the tomato puree and crushed tomatoes into the pot. Crumble in the oregano. Add the basil, salt, pepper, and 1½ cups water. Cook over low heat; stir occasionally.

After about 2 hours of slow cooking add the wine and blue claw crabs. Continue cooking 2 hours more, or until you see bits of white crab meat floating in the sauce.

Remove crabs to a separate platter. Ladle the sauce over the linguine and serve.

grilled striped bass *with* wasabi *and* ginger

keeper simple

GARY STUBER

In season I will fish relentlessly. When I am fortunate enough to bring home one of the local Bs—bass, blues, or bonito—a little white wine or sake, some tamari, and ginger brushed on while grilling makes fish disappear into thin air. I never marinate fish—it breaks down its structure and renders it soft. Let the fish flavor predominate. Keep it fresh and keep it simple! SERVES 10

the wasabi-ginger sauce
 ¼ cup toasted sesame oil
 ½ cup olive oil
 ¼ cup dry white wine
 2 tablespoons mirin
 4 tablespoons tamari sauce
 1 tablespoon finely grated fresh ginger
 2 teaspoons wasabi powder

 5 pounds striped bass fillets

Combine all sauce ingredients except the wasabi in a saucepan over medium-low heat. Stir and bring to a simmer, but do not boil. Whisk in the wasabi and cook until the sauce thickens (it should be pourable). Remove from the heat and set aside.

Place the bass fillets skin side down on a medium-high gas grill and brush liberally with sauce. Cook for about 10 minutes, brushing often with more sauce. Do not turn the fish over.

Remove the fish from the grill with a large spatula; the skin should remain on grill surface. Spoon remaining sauce over fillets and serve.

fava medley

MITZI PRATT

Fava beans love the maritime climate of the Vineyard and provide a bountiful harvest in mid-July if planted in early April. The plants and flowers are beautiful and the deer don't eat them. But they are laborious to prepare and my nod to the slow-food movement. On any given afternoon in midsummer a group of people, usually women, can be found shelling the pods on my porch above the garden. It has become a ritual I cherish as much as their good taste.

Have I mentioned that they freeze well? Simply put them in freezer bags after they've been blanched and slipped out of their skins (which make a lovely sound when dried). SERVES 6 TO 8

3 tablespoons olive oil
2 cloves garlic, finely chopped
1 zucchini, diced
2 summer squash, diced
3 cups fresh fava beans, shelled, blanched, and skinned (see note)
¼ cup chopped fresh herbs (marjoram and thyme are nice)
Juice of ½ lemon
½ teaspoon sea salt
¼ teaspoon freshly ground black pepper

Put the oil and garlic in a large skillet and cook over medium-high heat until the garlic is just shy of golden.

Remove the garlic from the oil with a spoon and put in a small bowl. Add the zucchini and squash to the skillet and cook until tender, about 3 minutes. Add the fava beans, garlic, and herbs and stir until the beans are heated.

Place in a serving bowl and stir in lemon juice, salt, and pepper.

Serve warm or at room temperature.

NOTE: To blanch fava beans, boil 2 quarts of water. Add the favas for 1 minute, remove, and rinse in cold water. Pinch the skins to break them and slip out the beans.

tamara's summer salad
gary's midnight salad dressing's better half

TAMARA WEISS

Salad is my absolute favorite food to make, to order in a restaurant, or to be served at a friend's house. I crave salad like a truck driver craves steak. I love it prepared a zillion ways, but my favorite salad is filled with fresh organic vegetables from one of the island's local farm stands. Any combination of greens will do, but color is mandatory. Salad is a meal unto itself, and splashed with a little of Gary's Midnight Salad Dressing, well, it's sublime. SERVES 8 TO 10

¾ cup sunflower seeds
1 tablespoon tamari sauce
2 bunches watercress (remove stems)
16 ounces mixed organic mesclun
¼ pound sugar snap peas, strings removed
3 ounces sunflower sprouts
2 organic Granny Smith apples, peeled and thinly sliced
2 ripe mangoes, peeled and sliced
1 cup peeled and grated organic carrots
1 ripe Hass avocado, peeled, pitted, and sliced

Heat a cast-iron skillet over medium heat. Add the sunflower seeds and toast them until they begin to brown.

Turn off the heat. Add the tamari and toss to coat all the seeds. Let cool.

In a large bowl (hopefully as pretty as your salad) combine the watercress, mesclun greens, sugar snap peas, and sunflower sprouts.

Now add color: apples, mangoes, carrots, and avocado.

Now add crunch: sprinkle the salad with toasted sunflower seeds.

Add some of Gary's Midnight Salad Dressing (the recipe follows) and toss just before serving.

gary's midnight salad dressing

the always-asked-for, what's-in-your-salad-dressing salad dressing

GARY STUBER

Cleaning up late at night after a big potluck dinner at our house is often an enjoyable experience because:

A. I'm alone in the kitchen with Tamara and we get to discuss the party.

B. There aren't as many dishes to wash because people take home what they brought.

C. I locate the salad bowl. If I am lucky, I'll find all the surprises that Tamara puts in her salad: sweet mango, smooth avocado, and crunchy sugar snap peas. Down at the bottom of the bowl, marinated in my always-asked-for, what's-in-my-salad-dressing salad dressing, is my midnight surprise. I grab a fork and do the only honorable thing. MAKES 1 QUART

1 sheet nori
1 cup olive oil
½ cup dry white wine (Chardonnay is nice)
1 cup balsamic vinegar
2 tablespoons tamari sauce
2 tablespoons Dijon mustard
4 cloves garlic, peeled
¼ cup apple cider
1 lemon, juiced
1 tablespoon grated lemon zest
Pinch of cayenne pepper
¼ tablespoon freshly ground black pepper

Toast the nori by holding the sheet with tongs over a medium flame and moving it back and forth until it crisps and turns slightly green.

Combine all the ingredients in a blender. Liquefy for approximately 3 minutes.

The dressing will keep for at least 3 days covered in the refrigerator. Bring it to room temperature before serving.

arroz verde

green is the color

LYNNE WHITING

Green is the color of my true love's eyes, the color of our living room walls, the summer fields where our animals graze. Each landscape, real or imagined on canvas, has green in it, somewhere. Earthy shades of green and beyond are woven together to form my wardrobe, while I view each sunny day through green-tinted lenses. Limeade and pistachios, baby spinach and crisp leafy lettuce, avocados and fresh cilantro, each one tempts my taste buds as well as my eyes. The color green nourishes me; it calms me and somehow helps me feel safe. It made perfect sense to bring Arroz Verde (Green Rice) to a gathering of friends, together to enjoy each other's kitchen creations. SERVES 4 TO 6

4 fresh poblano chiles (or substitute 4 green bell peppers, each 4 inches in diameter)
4 cups vegetable stock
1¼ cups coarsely chopped fresh parsley
½ cup coarsely chopped yellow onion
½ teaspoon peeled and finely chopped garlic
1 teaspoon salt
½ teaspoon freshly ground black pepper
¼ cup plus 2 tablespoons olive oil
2 cups raw long-grain rice
3 to 5 fresh-picked baby zucchinis, thinly sliced

Heat the oven to 350 degrees. Place the chiles on a baking sheet and roast until skins brown and the peppers are soft. Remove peppers from oven and wrap them in a damp towel. Let rest 5 minutes, then gently rub off their skins with the towel. Cut out stems and discard seeds. Chop into coarse chunks.

Combine 1 cup of chile chunks with ½ cup vegetable stock in blender. Blend at high speed for 15 seconds. Gradually add remaining chiles, 1 cup of the parsley, the onions, garlic, salt, and pepper. Blend until the mixture is reduced to a smooth puree.

Put ¼ cup olive oil into a 2- or 3-quart flameproof casserole and set over moderate heat. When oil is hot but not smoking, add the rice. Stir constantly for 2 to 3 minutes, until grains are well coated with oil and start to sound like pebbles. Add pureed chile mixture and simmer, stirring occasionally, for 5 minutes.

Meanwhile, bring the remaining 3½ cups of stock to a boil in a small saucepan. Pour the stock over the rice. Return to a boil, cover casserole, and reduce the heat to its lowest point. Simmer undisturbed for 18 to 20 minutes, until the rice is tender and has absorbed all of the liquid.

Sauté the zucchini in 2 tablespoons olive oil over medium-high heat until just tender.

Fluff the rice with a fork and garnish with the zucchini and remaining parsley. If the rice must wait, remove the lid and drape the pan loosely with a towel. Place in a 250-degree oven to keep warm.

nana's blueberry cake

KATE TAYLOR

My mother-in law, Jessie Witham (one of my baking mentors), used to lead blueberry-picking expeditions near her summer waterfront cottage. An average yield for such a trek would be three or four quarts of blueberries, from which she would produce blueberry pies, blueberry muffins, and blueberry cakes—all baked in a kerosene stove. Each week she would distribute the fruits of her labor to family, friends, and neighbors. It's a summer tradition that you will enjoy sharing with your loved ones. SERVES 12

¼ cup unsalted butter, at room temperature
1⅓ cups sugar, plus additional for coating
1 large egg, beaten until fluffy
2 cups unbleached all-purpose flour
2 tablespoons baking powder
½ teaspoon salt
½ cup milk
1½ cups blueberries
¼ teaspoon ground cinnamon
½ cup raspberries

Heat the oven to 350 degrees. Butter and flour a 9-inch round cake pan.

Beat the butter and 1 cup of sugar together in a large bowl until light. Beat in the egg.

In a separate bowl, mix 1¾ cups flour, the baking powder, and salt. Add the dry ingredients in three additions to the butter, alternating with the milk.

Toss 1 cup of blueberries with ¼ cup flour to coat. Fold into the batter. Scrape the batter into the pan. Combine the cinnamon with ⅓ cup sugar and sprinkle over the top of the cake.

Bake for 30 minutes (check at 20 minutes). You'll know it's done when a toothpick comes out clean. Cool on a rack.

Dip the remaining blueberries and raspberries in water, then roll them in sugar. Set aside to dry (approximately 15 minutes). When cake is cool, arrange sugared berries on top.

summer strawberry
and peach pie

PATRIE GRACE

My children love strawberries. When they were very small we would go to our local pick-your-own strawberry farm. I picked as quickly as possible, dreaming of jars of jam for holiday gifts and fresh berries for breakfast. Counting their full pails into the equation, I would turn to check our progress, only to find two of my four children plopped down by a plant, munching berry after berry, their pails empty. I had to laugh at their cheeks, mouths, and hands dripping juicy red. I'd wish I had brought a camera to capture the sweetness of the moment and the berries. We returned home with a somewhat meager amount one day to find a beautiful basket of peaches from our friends' Chilmark orchard with a note saying they'd stopped by. With many hands and the heavenly ingredients before us, we began the creation of our straw-berry and peach pie. MAKES 1 PIE

the filling
   3 cups fresh strawberries, hulled and sliced
   4 cups (about 1½ pounds) fresh peach slices
   ¾ to 1 cup organic turbinado sugar, plus 2 tablespoons for dusting
   2 teaspoons fresh lemon juice
   1 teaspoon grated lemon zest
   1 tablespoon minced crystallized ginger
   ¼ teaspoon ground allspice
   ¼ teaspoon nutmeg
   ¼ teaspoon salt
   3 or 4 tablespoons instant tapioca
   3 tablespoons unsalted butter

   1 (9-inch) piecrust (see page 234)

Combine all filling ingredients except the tapioca and butter in a large mixing bowl. Remove 1 cup of this mixture to a separate bowl and set aside. Now add the tapioca to the large bowl, stir, and let the mixture sit for 20 minutes.

Meanwhile, heat the oven to 350 degrees.

Pour the tapioca mixture into the prepared piecrust and spread it out evenly.

Spread the reserved cup of filling on top and dot with butter. To prevent over-browning, cover the edge of the pie with foil. Bake for 25 minutes.

Remove the foil and dust the top of the fruit with 2 tablespoons sugar and bake for 20 to 25 minutes more, until the fruit is bubbly and the crust is golden brown.

brownies *with* chocolate ganache

BETH KRAMER

My sister is the one in the family who most loves chocolate. (When we shared Oreos, she got the outside and I got the filling.) So my sister is my inspiration when it comes to most things chocolate. These brownies are elegant, easy to make, and satisfy even the most demanding chocolate lover. MAKES 20 BROWNIES

the brownies

  2 pounds semisweet chocolate, chopped
  1 cup (2 sticks) unsalted butter
  9 large eggs
  3 cups granulated sugar
  1 teaspoon vanilla extract
  ½ teaspoon salt
  3 cups all-purpose flour

the ganache

  3 cups heavy cream
  3 (12-ounce) packages semisweet chocolate chips

Heat the oven to 275 degrees. Prepare an 11×17-inch pan by spraying it with vegetable spray or spreading softened butter in the pan. Cover the bottom with a sheet of parchment paper.

To make the brownies, melt the chocolate and butter together in a heatproof bowl set over simmering water. Remove from the heat.

Whisk the eggs, sugar, and vanilla together in a large bowl until combined.

Sift the salt and flour together onto a piece of waxed paper.

Once the chocolate mixture has slightly cooled, add it to the egg mixture, whisking thoroughly. Add the flour mixture, stirring until completely combined.

Pour into the pan and bake for approximately 20 minutes until a cake tester comes out clean (test toward the edge of the pan rather than the middle of the brownies). Cool on a rack.

To make the ganache, bring the heavy cream just to a boil in a medium saucepan. Remove from the heat and whisk in the chocolate.

Once the brownies have thoroughly cooled, invert the pan over a cutting board and remove the parchment paper. Pour the ganache over the brownies, spread evenly with a spatula, and place in the refrigerator to set. Slice and serve once cooled.

AQUINNAH
lunch

The town of Aquinnah, formerly known as Gay Head, sits at the westernmost tip of the Vineyard. Aquinnah is the ancestral home of the Wampanoag Native Americans and one of the smallest towns in the state of Massachusetts. The magnificent clay cliffs (declared a National Landmark in 1966), 145-year-old lighthouse, and spectacular beaches are some of the most popular attractions on the Island. Tour buses unload and floods of day-trippers descend upon the gift shops, lured by the wampum bracelets, beaded belts, tomahawks, and T-shirts.

The Aquinnah Shop, the only restaurant in town, rests on the edge of the cliffs, commanding a breathtaking view of Noman's Land and the Elizabeth Islands. For some locals, the Aquinnah Shop is the center of town—where one goes to catch up on local gossip, politics, or fishing news. It is also where one might consume the freshest bluefish burger or strawberry rhubarb pie. As a young teen I waitressed at the Aquinnah Shop and will never forget that one of the requirements of the job was to memorize the ten or so varieties of pie homemade each day by proprietors Anne Vanderhoop and Luther Madison. During those summers my exposure to life in a small town left a lasting impression. My fondness and respect for Luther, a cook at Aquinnah and the Wampanoag tribe's medicine man, was such that years later, when Gary and I married, we asked Luther to preside over our wedding.

My parents moved from the sleepy village of Menemsha to the wilds of Gay Head in the 1960s. They were smart enough to buy land communally with a few of their friends. Forty-odd years later, they still enjoy their summer walks around the cliffs and daily swims in the cold North Shore, only now it is with their grandchildren at their side.

The original families who bought land together remain neighbors, and potluck gatherings are still the norm. Last August, that magical month when the afternoon sun casts a crimson light on the sea, my parents invited their neighbors and friends from up and down Lighthouse Road to a potluck luncheon on their deck. Some arrived barefoot from the beach, another on a motorcycle (pie in hand); others came Pied Piper–like down a secret path, whacking their way through rosehips and bullbriar, bearing cold ceviche, fresh baked bread, potato-mango salad, warm pie, and excellent wine. As usual at the Weiss table, the conversation flowed on topics as varied as which farm stand sold the biggest beets to world peace and disarmament. Fishing boats provided a backdrop, but the delicious food, good company, and ever-gentle breeze made for a perfect Aquinnah afternoon.

aquinnah bread

ANN LEONARD

The bread is baked. Warm loaf in hand, I walk the beach to supper with old friends. 2 ROUND LOAVES

  1 tablespoon dry active yeast
  1 tablespoon sugar
  2 cups lukewarm water
  1 tablespoon salt
  6 cups all-purpose flour (approximately)
  2 to 3 tablespoons cornmeal, for dusting baking sheet
  Sesame or poppy seeds (optional)

Combine the yeast, sugar, and water in a large mixing bowl. Let sit until bubbles form. Add the salt and the flour, 1 cup at a time. Knead briefly. Place the dough in a large well-oiled bowl, cover with a warm, damp cloth, and let rise until the dough doubles in size. It takes approximately 50 minutes to rise.

Sprinkle a baking sheet with the cornmeal.

Punch down the dough and form into two balls. Set the balls of dough on the cornmeal, cover again with a warm, damp cloth, and let the loaves rise for 5 minutes.

Slash the tops of the loaves, using a sharp knife, with three diagonal lines. Brush the loaves with water and, if desired, sprinkle the tops with sesame or poppy seeds.

Set the baking sheet in a cold oven. Place a pan of hot water underneath the rack of bread. Turn the oven to 400 degrees and bake for 40 minutes.

This bread is at its most delicious the first day. If, by chance, you have any left over it makes excellent toast, French toast, or bread pudding.

chlodnik

GLORIA LEVITAS

Chlodnik means "cool" in Polish, and it is, to my mind, the perfect soup for a hot summer's day. Mixing crisp cucumbers, sweet beets, creamy yogurt, spicy radishes, garlic, and scallions with sprightly dill, it is the color of a summer sunset. This soup makes a wonderful first course at dinner, or a complete meal at lunch when served with a sandwich or a fish and bean salad.

A wonderful Polish journalist who visits Aquinnah from time to time gave me the basic recipe. I have altered it slightly both to suit my tastes and in accordance with the availability of the ingredients in my larder. Living in Aquinnah, a considerable distance from the nearest grocery store, I often substitute ingredients or omit some from familiar dishes. The results, more often than not, are dishes even more interesting than the originals.

(Gloria Levitas, a summer resident of Aquinnah since 1964, is an anthropologist with a specialty in the cultural analysis of food.) SERVES 6

2 beets, scrubbed or peeled, quartered
1 cucumber, sliced in half lengthwise and seeded
1 carrot, peeled and cut into chunks
1 green apple, peeled, cored, and cut into chunks
1 clove garlic, minced
2 scallions, finely chopped
8 ounces plain yogurt (low- or nonfat)
16 ounces buttermilk
½ teaspoon sour salt (you can use the contents of 2 vitamin C capsules, or a teaspoon of lemon juice, to substitute for the sour salt)
1 teaspoon sea salt
1 tablespoon sugar or honey
3 tablespoons fresh dill, chopped
3 radishes, finely chopped
2 hard-cooked eggs, coarsely chopped

Place the beets in a saucepan and cover them with water. Salt the water and bring to a boil. Cook covered for about 20 minutes over medium heat, until tender. Remove the beets with a slotted spoon. Reserve 1 cup of the cooking liquid.

Put the beets, reserved cooking liquid, cucumber, carrot, apple, garlic, and half the scallions in a blender or food processor and mix until liquefied.

Add the yogurt and buttermilk and mix again, until well combined. Next add the sour salt, sea salt, and sugar. Adjust the seasonings to your taste. Mix again.

Ladle the chlodnik into soup bowls and sprinkle with dill, chopped radishes, remaining scallions, and eggs as a garnish just before serving. You can also top each bowl with a dollop of sour cream—or add grated carrots, as we did for the photograph. This soup is delicious at room temperature or chilled. Try it with a fresh-baked loaf of rye bread, or Ann Leonard's Aquinnah Bread (see page 79).

brie *and* apricot canapés

R I T A   L L O Y D

brought by gloria levitas

Rita Lloyd is a frequent guest of Gloria and Mike Levitas. She is an actress who has appeared in such television programs as The Guiding Light, As the World Turns, *and* The Edge of Night *as well as in numerous off-Broadway and regional theater productions. You may well have heard her documentary narrations and voiceovers. Rita operated a catering business, Rita Lloyd and Company, in New York City for several years.*

These canapés are simple to make and can be made ahead of time, frozen, and browned in a toaster oven or under your broiler just before serving. Wonderful.

MAKES 48 CANAPÉS

½ loaf thin-sliced Pepperidge Farm bread (if you can't find thin-sliced bread, buy an unsliced white loaf and cut into ¼-inch slices, or press ordinary slices flat with the side of a cleaver)
Dijon mustard
16 apricots, cut or chopped into small pieces
⅓ pound brie cheese (let it stand on the counter for 1 hour)

Cut each slice of bread with a 1-inch round cookie cutter into 4 rounds. Lightly toast the rounds on one side. (This is best done by placing the rounds on trays and using the top-brown setting of your toaster oven. If you don't have a toaster oven, you can use your oven broiler, but you will have to watch the bread carefully so that it doesn't burn.)

Spread each toasted round with about ⅓ teaspoon Dijon mustard. Lay the apricots over the mustard and cover with a slice of brie. If you are going to serve the canapés immediately, place them in a toaster oven and set to top-brown. Remove when the brie is bubbling.

To reserve for later use, cover the trays with foil and place canapés in the freezer. To serve, remove the trays from the freezer and place in toaster oven as directed above.

You can make variations of this hors d'oeuvre using brie with mustard and chutney, chopped olives or olive paste, sun-dried tomatoes, or ham. You can also substitute a dark German rye bread for a different-tasting canapé.

ceviche

PATRIE GRACE

SERVES 10

1 pound medium shrimp, peeled and
   deveined
¼ teaspoon saffron threads
1 cup clam juice
½ pound scallops, coarsely chopped
¾ cup fresh orange juice
½ cup fresh lime juice
2 tablespoons finely chopped red
   onion
2 tablespoons coarsely chopped
   seedless yellow tomatoes
2 tablespoons chopped scallions
2 tablespoons chopped cilantro, plus
   extra leaves for garnish
1 small red jalapeño chile, seeded and
   chopped
1 small green jalapeño chile, seeded
   and chopped
¾ teaspoon aji amarillo yellow chile
   paste
Sea salt, to taste
1 teaspoon hot pepper sauce

Cook the shrimp in 2 quarts of boiling salted water over high heat for 3 minutes. Drain and submerge the shrimp in a bowl of ice water for 5 minutes. Drain again and chop coarsely.

Toast the saffron in a dry skillet for 1 minute on medium heat. Stir in the clam juice and simmer. Reduce to ½ cup (this will take 5 to 6 minutes, simmering). Pour into a large, nonmetallic bowl. Let cool.

Combine the shrimp, scallops, and orange and lime juices with the clam juice reduction. Cover and refrigerate for 3 hours, stirring occasionally. Add the rest of the ingredients (leaving the cilantro leaves for garnish) and toss. If the salad has too much liquid, pour off some of the marinade juices.

Garnish with cilantro. Serve chilled.

helen's greek meatballs
keftedes

HELEN MILONAS

The Greek meatballs almost became a Greek tragedy. It was our twenty-fifth year of summering in the Old Manter Farmhouse in West Tisbury, and I was preparing days in advance to host a large party for a friend where Greek hors d'oeuvre were to be the highlight. I had prepared more than 300 meatballs, anticipating freezing and then cooking them the morning of the party. Along came Hurricane Bob and so began several days without electricity. Chief George Manter came to my rescue with a generator with enough power to freeze the meatballs (and flush the toilets!). On the morning of the party I ended up having to barbecue the meatballs, but they turned out delicious. People were thrilled to be out of confinement, and the Greek party was a success. MAKES APPROXIMATELY 50 COCKTAIL MEATBALLS

1 to 2 slices white sandwich bread (crusts removed)
½ cup milk
2 pounds ground beef
1 large onion, finely chopped
4 or 5 cloves garlic, finely chopped
½ bunch flat-leaf parsley, finely chopped
1 tablespoon dried Greek oregano
2 tablespoons olive oil
1½ tablespoons wine vinegar
Juice of 2 limes
1 to 2 ounces ouzo or vodka
Salt and freshly ground black pepper, to taste
Olive oil, for frying
½ cup flour

Place the bread in a shallow bowl, pour the milk on top, and let sit for a few minutes. Squeeze the milk out of the soaked bread.

Combine the soaked bread with the rest of the ingredients, except the frying oil and the flour. Work the mixture with your hands so that the meat incorporates the other ingredients.

Cover the bowl with plastic wrap and refrigerate for a few hours or overnight. After the mixture has chilled, remove it from the refrigerator and make cocktail-

size meatballs. Place approximately 1 tablespoon of the meat mixture on your palm and roll it, with your other hand, into a ball. Place rolled balls on a board or tray. Continue making meatballs until the entire mixture is used.

Heat 1 inch of olive oil in a large frying pan. Dip your hands in the flour and roll meatballs lightly so that each one is coated with the flour, then place the balls into the heated oil. (The oil will sizzle when the meatballs are put in the pan; if it doesn't, the oil isn't hot enough.)

Fry the meatballs in small batches and keep turning until they are evenly browned and crisp on the outside. When they are cooked through remove them with a slotted spoon. Place the cooked Greek meatballs on a tray lined with paper towels to absorb any excess oil. Transfer to a serving platter. Serve at room temperature or reheat in the oven just before serving.

shark bait

braised brisket sandwiches for poker

JESSE BROWNER

For some twelve years now, I have hosted a permanent floating poker game for friends, acquaintances, and would-be sharks. In that time, I've learned that, no matter what Neil Simon might say on the subject, poker players are neither oblivious nor hostile to the charms of a decent meal. In fact, they tend to be particularly appreciative, since they are so rarely catered to in the fashion to which they would like to become accustomed.

In my years of cooking for gamblers, I have learned what all great chefs of the world are born knowing: The true purpose of good cooking is not to entertain, impress, or satisfy your guests, but to manipulate those weaker than you. This very sound principle can be exploited to great advantage at the poker table. Find the crustiest, most fragrant roll you can; burden it with four generous wedges of buttery brisket; drown them in rich horseradish gravy; serve with a dill pickle, thick-cut potato chips, and a yeasty Dutch lager; then watch your friends, who are generally suspicious and monitor your every move as the lamb monitors the wolf, abandon all their wise caution and make mistake after reckless mistake at the gaming table. Don't kid yourself—there is nothing unethical about it. This is why we cook, to lull our guests into the illusion of an easier world, if only for an hour or two. They want you to do it to them, they expect you to try, and they hope beyond hope that you succeed. Being skinned of next week's rent is a small price to pay for this experience, and they know it. That's why they keep coming back.

The following recipe, by the way, can be readily adapted to less aggressive venues, such as brunches, church picnics, ice hockey tournaments, and the like, by resorting to the alternatives supplied in the note at the end of the recipe.

MAKES 12 SANDWICHES

2 tablespoons vegetable oil
Salt and freshly ground black pepper
1 (4- to 5-pound) brisket

2 medium onions, coarsely chopped
1 small can tomato paste
4 cups beef or chicken stock (or 2 cups water
    and 2 cups red wine, or 4 cups water)
1 tablespoon prepared horseradish
1 tablespoon Dijon mustard
12 hard rolls (Kaiser or Portuguese)

Heat the oven to 325 degrees.

Heat the oil in a heavy-bottomed casserole dish over medium heat. Salt and pepper the brisket, then brown it slowly on all sides. Remove the brisket from the pan and set it on a wooden board or kitchen plate.

Sauté the onions to a golden brown in the casserole. Return the brisket to the casserole dish and add the tomato paste and liquid of choice to barely cover, heating to a low simmer. Cover the casserole and place in the oven for 2½ hours. Uncover the brisket and cook for another 30 minutes. The meat should be extremely tender.

Remove the brisket to a carving board. Allow it to rest 15 minutes, then carve it into thin slices.

While the brisket is resting transfer the braising liquid to a mixing bowl and place it in the freezer for 20 minutes. Remove from the freezer and skim off all the fat that has risen to the surface. Return the liquid to the casserole dish, bring it to a fast boil, and reduce the liquid by half.

Whisk in the horseradish and mustard. Transfer the reduced sauce to a gravy boat.

Slice your rolls in half lengthwise and lay the brisket slices on the rolls (figure 3 or 4 slices for each). Either pour the sauce on top and serve, or invite your guests to sauce their own sandwiches to taste.

NOTE: For a more elegant presentation, place thin slices of brisket on squares of white or pumpernickel bread. Top with a small dollop of crème fraîche whisked with prepared horseradish.

green beans *with* roasted pecan dressing

PATRIE GRACE

SERVES 10

1 tablespoon coarse salt
2 pounds haricots verts (green beans), topped and tailed
½ cup pecans, roasted (see note, below)
½ cup flat-leaf parsley, coarsely chopped
½ cup cilantro, coarsely chopped
3 cloves garlic, peeled and minced
Juice of 4 lemons
5 tablespoons pink peppercorns, crushed, for garnish

Fill a large saucepan with water, salt it, and bring to a boil. Add the haricots verts, cooking until bright green and tender, 3 to 4 minutes.

Drain the haricots verts and rinse them in cold water. Place in your serving dish.

Put the roasted pecans, parsley, cilantro, garlic, and lemon juice in a food processor and mix until all ingredients are well combined (it will be thick). If you like, you can make the dressing thinner by adding 2 or 3 tablespoons of water.

Spoon the dressing out of the processor and onto the green beans, then toss together. Sprinkle with the pink peppercorns and serve at room temperature, or, on a hot summer's day, refrigerate for an hour or more and serve chilled.

NOTE: To pan-roast pecans (or any nut), place them in a big skillet over medium heat, shaking the pan and stirring until the nuts are golden brown and fragrant. Transfer the nuts to a bowl or plate and let them cool.

potato *and* cucumber salad *with* mango salsa

CORA WEISS

Summer comfort. Golden smooth mangoes, crunchy fresh cucumbers, satisfying young potatoes combine with enough spike to make a Vineyard lunch. The right colors and textures sit well with the Sound view of the Elizabeths on a sunny day to hold you happily until sunset. For forty-four years we have been combining fruits and vegetables and eating on the deck, with a lovely Aussie Chardonnay and Pellegrino. Those are among the memories that keep us warm all winter and bring us back every year. No matter where we may roam during the year, Aquinnah is a magnet in August. SERVES 10

the salad
    20 small Yukon gold potatoes, scrubbed
    1 English cucumber
    1 Kirby cucumber
    1 cup cherry tomatoes, sliced in half
    5 mint sprigs, chopped, plus another for garnish
    5 fresh cilantro leaves, finely chopped
    1/2 teaspoon finely chopped fresh tarragon
    1/2 lime

the salsa
    3 ripe mangoes, peeled, pitted, and diced (reserve 1 slice for garnish)
    1 red bell pepper, seeded and diced
    1 yellow bell pepper, seeded and diced
    1 poblano chile, seeded and diced
    1 tomatillo, seeded and diced
    2 red scallions (small red onions), diced
    2 limes
    1/2 teaspoon cumin powder
    1/4 teaspoon red chili powder
    1 cup rice wine vinegar (garlic flavor)

To make the salad, steam the potatoes 15 to 20 minutes, or until tender when pierced with a fork. When cooled peel the potatoes and cut them into quarters.

Peel the cucumbers, leaving some green, cut them in half lengthwise, remove the seeds, then cut in ½-inch slices. Mix the cucumbers with the potatoes and cherry tomatoes in a large salad bowl.

Toss the chopped mint, cilantro, and tarragon over the cucumber, tomato, and potato mixture. Squeeze the lime over the entire bowl and cover. Refrigerate until chilled, at least 1 hour.

To make the salsa, combine the diced mangoes, peppers, poblano, tomatillo, and red scallions in a small mixing bowl. Squeeze the juice of 1 lime over all and toss well.

Mix the cumin, red chili powder, and rice wine vinegar in another small mixing bowl. Pour this mixture over the mango mixture, toss together, then add more lime juice to taste. Refrigerate until chilled, at least 1 hour.

Just before serving, pour the salsa mixture over the potato and cucumber salad and toss gently until thoroughly mixed. Add sliced mango and mint sprig on top for decoration.

mitzu's silken tofu *and* shrimp

AS INTERPRETED BY EMILY DAVIDSON

This dish can be served as an appetizer, a first course, or a luncheon dish with other salads. A Japanese friend gave me this recipe. He is also a hair stylist with his own salon in New York City.

I have used more of everything because I am bringing the dish for lunch, but the first time I made it I used only ¼ pound of shrimp, one package of tofu, and small spoonfuls of all the other ingredients. So you may adapt this recipe in many different ways, which is the way I like to cook on Martha's Vineyard. I am only exact when I bake. SERVES 8

2 silken tofu, cut in about ½-inch squares
1½ pounds medium shrimp, shelled, boiled until done (2 to 3 minutes), and chopped
1 red bell pepper, finely chopped
1 yellow bell pepper, finely chopped
1 bunch scallions, green and white parts, finely chopped
14 basil leaves, chopped, plus extra leaves for garnish
1 tablespoon sugar
¼ cup sesame oil
¼ cup finely grated fresh ginger
⅛ cup rice vinegar
¼ cup soy sauce
1 jalapeño pepper, seeded then finely chopped

Mix all of the ingredients together in a large salad bowl. Toss until well combined. Refrigerate for at least 5 hours and up to 24 hours. Garnish with basil leaves and serve.

lighthouse lasagna

ELEANOR JOHNSON

Every summer, for just a few weeks, we escape to the Vineyard, home of old child-hood haunts and memories. Lighthouse Lasagna is a somewhat glamorous name for a solid, reliable dish that is impervious to food trends. My mother served it through-out my childhood, through all the seasons, and now, for our three boys, it's the one meal they can all agree on. Summers come and go, but this dish lives on!

SERVES 8

    1 pound ground round
    1 small can tomato paste
    1 (8-ounce) can tomato sauce
    1 teaspoon sugar
    Coarse salt
    12 ounces egg noodles
    1 tablespoon unsalted butter
    1 cup sour cream
    3 ounces cream cheese, at room temperature
    1 bunch scallions, finely chopped
    8 ounces cheddar cheese, sliced

Heat the oven to 350 degrees.

Sauté the meat until lightly browned in a large skillet over medium heat, breaking it up as it cooks. Add the tomato paste, tomato sauce, and sugar. Fill the tomato paste can with water and stir it in. Simmer, covered, for 15 to 20 minutes.

Fill a large pot with water, salt it, and bring it to a boil. Add the egg noodles and cook them until tender. Drain the noodles, then return them to the pot. Stir in the butter.

Mix the sour cream, cream cheese, and scallions in a small bowl. Make two layers of the ingredients in a large casserole dish, as follows: Spread a little sauce over the bottom of the dish, top with a layer of noodles, then spread half of the sour cream mixture and half of the meat sauce. Repeat these steps. Top the lasagna with the sliced cheddar.

Bake for 45 to 50 minutes, until the lasagna mixture is bubbly and the cheese is lightly browned.

the ultimate watercress salad *with* champagne dressing

PATRIE GRACE

SERVES 6

the dressing
1 cup champagne vinegar
2 tablespoons sugar
1½ tablespoons unbleached flour
2 teaspoons dry vermouth
1 teaspoon Dijon mustard
1 large egg, beaten
3 tablespoons heavy cream
2 cups olive oil
Sea salt and freshly ground black pepper

the salad
2 pounds fresh watercress, rinsed well
4 ounces chèvre (fresh goat cheese)
¾ cup walnuts, roasted (see page 89)
4 ripe kiwis, peeled and cut into ¼-inch slices
1 ripe mango, peeled and sliced off the pit

To make the dressing, combine the vinegar, sugar, flour, vermouth, and mustard in a small saucepan. Simmer over medium heat, stirring continuously.

Slowly whisk in the egg and cream over low heat. Whisk in the olive oil in a thin, steady stream. Season with salt and pepper to taste.

This makes 3 cups and keeps well in the refrigerator for a few days.

To make the salad, remove stems from the watercress, tear it into pieces, and place in bowl. Crumble the goat cheese with your hands on top of the greens. Toss in the roasted walnuts. Spread the kiwis and mangoes on top in your own creative fashion. Any vinaigrette will complement this salad, but try it with the Champagne Dressing.

raspberry tart

CLAUDIA WEILL AND WALTER TELLER

Pies have long been a hot topic of conversation on the Vineyard. On beaches and at dinners, the vigorous debate continues year after year as to whose pie has the flakiest crust, the freshest fruit, the proper amount of pectin or sugar. This isn't to say that fishing, land development, conservation, traffic, mopeds, and other issues aren't also serious concerns, but pies are quite correctly of paramount interest. For many, a dinner (and even a breakfast or lunch) without pie is, as they say, like a day without sunshine.

This raspberry tart has a lot to recommend it. It is larger, flatter, more colorful, easier to make, and less fragile than most, but it still satisfies the pie urge. It is fun to make alone or with company. It looks fantastic and tastes even better, with the purity of the fruit and the sweet crunchiness of the crust in perfect balance. Most important, it travels better resting on the tank of a motorcycle than a conventional pie. We adapted this from a recipe in The Barefoot Contessa Cookbook.

SERVES 10 TO 12

the tart shell
   ³⁄₄ cup (1½ sticks) unsalted butter, at room temperature
   ½ cup sugar
   ½ teaspoon pure vanilla extract
   1¾ cups all-purpose flour, plus extra for dusting work surface
   Pinch salt

   1 cup good raspberry preserves
   1½ pints (3 packages) fresh raspberries

Heat the oven to 350 degrees.

To make the tart shell, mix the butter and sugar in the bowl of an electric mixer fitted with a paddle attachment. Beat until the ingredients are just combined. Add the vanilla and mix for another minute. Sift together the flour and salt into a medium bowl. Add the flour mixture to the butter and sugar mixture and mix on low speed until the dough begins to come together.

Dust your work surface and turn the dough onto it. Shape dough into a flat disk. Press the dough disk into a 10-inch round removable bottom tart pan.

Trim excess dough from sides, making sure the finished edge is flat. Chill until firm.

Butter one side of a 10-inch square of aluminum foil. Place buttered side down on chilled tart. Cover the foil with dried beans and bake the shell for 20 minutes. Remove the foil and the beans and prick the tart all over with the tines of a fork. Bake again for 20 minutes more, until lightly browned. Cool to room temperature.

To fill the tart, spread the cooled tart shell with the raspberry preserves, then place the fresh raspberries, stem end down, in concentric circles on top. Serve immediately.

INDIAN
night

It was autumn when Francesca Kelly first blew through the doors of Midnight Farm. I was sitting at my desk behind the old glass window that separates my office from the rest of the world. I looked up and couldn't help but stare at her as she circled the room like a ballet teacher checking the posture of her students.

She was wearing tan riding boots laced to her knees. A brown pashmina shawl draped over one shoulder and was belted tightly at her slender waist. Her hair, pulled back in a bun, showed off her elegant features and beautiful jewelry. Large gold cuffs peered out from the sleeves of her jacket, hugging her wrists.

I remember being drawn out onto the floor as if witnessing a small tornado gathering speed. Was there a Ralph Lauren photo shoot going on in Vineyard Haven? "Lovely store," came the voice beneath the pashmina. I detected an English accent. I introduced myself, she firmly shook my hand, and was gone. Two days later Francesca returned, blowing in the same gale force as before, only this time accompanied by her husband, James, and two teenage daughters, Amber and Melisande. This time she stayed. As she rifled through clothing, smelled candles, and browsed the book table, I did what I often do and extracted as much information from her as humanly possible in a retail moment.

She lived in England, she told me, traveled much of the year to India, and recently built a house by the sea on Chappaquiddick. Her passion: a rare breed of Indian horses called Marwari.

That brief encounter took place a couple of years ago, and Gary and I now count Francesca and James among our dearest Island friends. Recently, they traded in their London town house for life year-round on Chappy. Francesca still spends much of the year traveling throughout northern India, where she is known as *Ghoravalli,* "she who rides horses." She has entered and won (the only woman ever to do so) some of India's top endurance races. Her dream is to introduce the Marwari, with their lyre-shaped ears and fiery eyes, to the West.

Francesca's other passion is dancing. Any excuse to gather people under her roof for the sole purpose of jumping around barefoot on the wooden floor is a welcome one. She suggested an Indian potluck dinner to bid farewell to summer and to welcome the oncoming fall. On Labor Day weekend, when most of the summer visitors return to their other lives, one can actually feel the Island rise in the sea. The other island, Chappaquiddick, off the Edgartown harbor, is a unique destination for those who rarely find the time to venture there.

Ethnic food on Martha's Vineyard is hard to come by, but guests rose to the challenge of dreaming something up other than corn on the cob, green salad, or bluefish. One thinks of spices when dreaming of Indian cuisine, and much to my surprise, almost everything needed for this feast was available right here in our local markets. Upon entering Lammastide, as James and Francesca's house is named, one has the feeling of entering a giant barn or the belly of a boat filled with wood, ancient Indian textiles, flowers, candles, clay, and stone. There is a noticeable absence of the outside world—no television, ringing telephone, newspapers, junk mail, or plastic of any kind. Lammastide has the feeling of a beautiful spiritual retreat.

Color ruled the night of the potluck—burnt orange, hot fuchsia, crimson red, saffron yellow. It was everywhere: in the food, our clothing, and the waning summer sky. There was an Indian sunset that night on Chappaquiddick, and it cast a glow on Lammastide that warmed our hearts and set fire to our dancing feet.

green mango chutney

JOE NORRIS

SERVES 8

2 green mangoes, peeled and chopped in $\frac{1}{2}$-inch chunks
Juice of 3 to 4 limes
2 cloves garlic, peeled
2 medium yellow onions, chopped
2 tablespoons grated fresh ginger
1 bunch parsley, washed and stems removed
1 bunch mint, washed and stems removed
3 green chiles
3 tablespoons mild olive oil
1 tablespoon sugar, or more if needed
1 pinch salt

Toss the green mangoes with the juice of 1 lime in a medium bowl and set aside.

Place the remaining ingredients—including the juice of 2 limes—in a food processor. Coarsely chop by pulsing the processor so as *not* to puree. Scoop out the mixture into the bowl of mangoes and toss. Taste for a balance of sweet and sour and adjust with more lime juice or sugar if needed.

stir-fried sugar snaps

FRANCESCA KELLY

This is a fast and simple dish, and you can use practically any vegetable. We used sugar snap peas for the color. Chiles are optional. SERVES 6

3 tablespoons olive oil
½ teaspoon brown mustard seeds
1½ pounds fresh sugar snap peas
6 fresh green chiles (or red), seeds removed and sliced into long slivers (optional)
¼ teaspoon ground turmeric
½ teaspoon ground coriander
½ teaspoon lime juice
Salt, to taste

Heat the oil in a large cast-iron wok over medium heat. When it is sizzling, add the mustard seeds; as soon as they pop add all the other ingredients and stir-fry them for 2 to 3 minutes, stirring constantly. Remove from the heat and serve immediately.

sweet potato *and* basil

JOE NORRIS

SERVES 4 TO 6

2 to 3 tablespoons ghee (or clarified butter)
1 teaspoon ground cumin
1 teaspoon ground coriander
1 teaspoon ground turmeric
1 pinch ground cardamom
1 pound sweet potatoes, peeled and cut into ¼-inch slices
5 sprigs of fresh basil
Salt and freshly ground black pepper

Heat the ghee in a large, heavy-bottomed pot on medium heat. Add the cumin, coriander, turmeric, and cardamom and briefly sauté over medium heat, until the spices are slightly toasted and aromatic. Now add the sweet potatoes and cook until lightly browned. Pour in enough water to cover the sweet potatoes. Cover the pot and continue cooking until all the water is absorbed and the potatoes are tender. This takes about 15 minutes.

Slice the basil into thin ribbon strips and fold into the cooked potatoes. Season with salt and pepper to taste. Serve warm.

beetroot salad

FRANCESCA KELLY

I put this together to offset the palette of browns and yellows that characterizes Indian cooking. SERVES 12

6 large beets, scrubbed or peeled, then grated
3 carrots, grated
1 tablespoon grated fresh ginger
1 pound fresh bean sprouts
Juice of 1 lime
¼ cup olive oil
Dash of maple syrup
1 teaspoon caraway seeds
1 bunch fresh coriander, chopped, for garnish

Mix the beets, carrots, ginger, and bean sprouts (which will, of course, turn pink) in a salad bowl. Toss in the lime juice, olive oil, maple syrup, and caraway seeds. Garnish with the fresh coriander leaves and some chive flowers or other blue flowers to cool the palate. This salad is well complemented with a mint or cucumber raita (see page 110).

coriander chicken

FRANCESCA KELLY

This is really a wonderful southern Indian dish bursting with flavors. Sometimes I'll leave out the chiles for a sweeter, milder flavor and add extra cardamom. Once you've prepared the marinade it only takes 30 minutes to cook and serve, and even people who are not wild about Indian food will love it. (Better leave the chiles out altogether for them.) SERVES 6 TO 8

the marinade
1 teaspoon ground cloves
1 teaspoon ground cardamom
$\frac{1}{2}$ teaspoon ground bay leaves
$\frac{1}{2}$ teaspoon ground cinnamon
2 tablespoons ground coriander
1 cup plain yogurt

$2\frac{1}{2}$ pounds chicken thighs and breasts
5 tablespoons mustard oil (or substitute olive oil)
1 pinch ground asafetida (can be found in an ethnic food store)
3 cups chopped cilantro
1 teaspoon sugar
6 fresh hot green chiles, sliced (optional)

Mix all the marinade ingredients in a large bowl and then add the chicken pieces. Refrigerate overnight or for at least 2 hours prior to cooking. Remove the chicken from the marinade and put the marinade aside. Heat the mustard oil in a large, heavy pan or wok on medium heat. When hot add the asafetida and let it sizzle for a few seconds. Turn the heat to high and add all the chicken, stirring and frying for 10 to 15 minutes until the chicken is browned. Add the marinade, cilantro (leave some for garnish), and sugar. Keep stirring and frying over medium heat until the chicken is tender. Add the chiles, if using, and stir until they soften. Reduce the heat to low and simmer until the sauce is thick. Serve plain or on a bed of rice and sprinkle with fresh cilantro.

raita

BROOKE ADAMS

With its cooling taste and color, this wonderful salad is an excellent accompaniment to any Indian dish. SERVES 6

5 to 6 medium cucumbers, peeled, seeded, and finely chopped
2 cups minced white onion
1½ teaspoons minced green chile (serrano, Thai, or jalapeño)
5 cups low-fat plain yogurt
1½ teaspoons ground cumin
1 pinch cayenne pepper
1 pinch freshly ground black pepper
2 teaspoons salt

Combine all of the ingredients in a medium bowl. The raita can be served immediately or refrigerated for 1 to 2 hours, then served chilled.

uppity down island
lobster mayonnaise

NANCY ELLISON

This elegant summer stunner, taught to me by the fabulous, eccentric chef Dione Lucas, is indeed "vieux cuisine." While originally designed for formal presentations, it adapts brilliantly for summer on the Vineyard. The flavor is guaranteed! The art is in the assembly. SERVES 6 TO 8

3 (1-pound) lobsters, boiled
4 cups coarsely chopped green beans
1 large onion, sliced
3 large cucumbers (peel if waxed), coarsely chopped
4 stalks celery, sliced
5 carrots, sliced
1 cup cooked rice, chilled
About ½ cup vinaigrette (use your favorite)
½ cup mayonnaise, flavored with a touch of curry powder
2 tablespoons light cream
1 tablespoon paprika
½ bunch watercress, for garnish

Shell the lobsters and reserve the meat of one tail as a garnish. Wash, dry, and oil one perfect fantail and one lobster head; reserve these as a garnish. Chop the rest of the lobster meat coarsely.

Mix the green beans, onion, cucumbers, celery, carrots, chopped lobster meat, and rice in a large bowl. Toss with the vinaigrette, adding it slowly to taste. Place the salad on an oval serving dish, molding it with your hands into a cleanly defined mound. Thin the mayonnaise with the cream and then pour it over the salad mound, covering it evenly. Sprinkle with the paprika and garnish the edges with watercress.

Slice the reserved lobster tail lengthwise, then place it on top of the mound. It should lie flat and look like a lobster tail. Place the oiled lobster head at one end of the mound and the fantail at the other, visually reassembling the lobster on top. Cover your creation with plastic wrap and refrigerate for at least 1 hour before serving.

grilled striped bass *with* papaya-lime sauce

JAIME HAMLIN

I love Asian food: Thai, Japanese, Chinese, Indian, or Pacific Rim. These exotic and varied flavors are an unending discovery of new tastes.

This is a recipe I invented that combines a stellar and seasonal Vineyard fish, striped bass, with some traditional Indian spices. Serve it with jasmine rice, pappadams and a salad; it's perfect for a special summer dinner. SERVES 6

the marinade
½ cup canola oil (or vegetable oil)
2 tablespoons grated fresh ginger
3 cloves garlic
1 tablespoon curry powder
1 tablespoon whole roasted cumin seeds (see note)
¼ teaspoon red pepper flakes
½ teaspoon salt

1 (3-pound) striped bass

the sauce
1 tablespoon canola oil
4 tablespoons chopped garlic
4 tablespoons grated fresh ginger
1 serrano chile, chopped finely
1 teaspoon curry powder
1 cup plain yogurt
1 papaya, peeled, seeded, and chopped
¼ cup mango chutney (Major Grey's is good)
¼ cup fresh lime juice
2 tablespoons roasted cumin seeds
1 tablespoon salt

To make the marinade, combine all the marinade ingredients in a small bowl. Place the bass in a shallow glass baking dish and pour the marinade over the fish. Refrigerate and marinate for 6 hours or overnight.

To make the sauce, put the canola oil in a small skillet over medium heat. Add the garlic, ginger, and chile and sauté for 2 to 3 minutes. Add the curry powder and sauté for another 2 minutes. Combine the yogurt, papaya, chutney, lime juice, cumin seeds, salt, and the sautéed garlic mixture in a food processor and process until smooth. Don't be afraid to adjust the flavors to suit your taste.

Prepare the grill and remove the fish from the marinade. Grill over a medium-hot flame for about 7 minutes per side, depending on the thickness of the fish. Place the grilled bass on a serving platter and drizzle some of the sauce over it. Garnish with fresh lime wedges and slices of papaya, or fresh rose petals. Pour the remaining sauce in a sauceboat and pass around with the fish.

NOTE: Roast the cumin seeds in a small, dry skillet over medium heat, shaking the pan, for approximately 2 minutes.

chickpea salad

JILL AMADO

I grew up surrounded by three sisters and a mother who did not cook. My grand-mother Marbie, who lived with us from the time I was born, taught me everything I know about cooking. My first memories of cooking are of standing on a footstool at her side rolling out piecrust. From that moment on, I knew that cooking was my ultimate passion. As most of us who have lived on the Island for more than twenty years know, winter journeys are of the utmost importance. I love to return with new recipes and exotic creations from faraway lands. I'm always up for the challenge of a good Martha's Vineyard potluck. SERVES 12

the salad
    1 medium red bell pepper
    1 medium red onion
    2 stalks celery
    2 carrots
    1 bunch cilantro
    2 (15-ounce) cans chickpeas, drained and rinsed

the dressing
    ¼ cup olive oil
    2 tablespoons red wine vinegar
    2 tablespoons cumin powder
    Salt and freshly ground black
        pepper, to taste

To make the salad, wash and finely chop all the vegetables and the cilantro. Toss them with the chick-peas in a large salad bowl.

To make the dressing, whisk together the dressing ingredients. Pour over the chickpeas and vegetables. Chill for at least 1 hour. Serve, garnishing with extra cilantro or nasturtiums, squash blossoms, or marigolds.

mango lassi

FRANCESCA KELLY

After a few weeks of desert camps, dust-flavored dahl, no sugar, and accelerated cravings for Thanksgiving dinners, my greatest indulgence is to sit in the cool gardens of one of Rajasthan's beautiful palaces sipping a large fruit lassi. A good lassi should be savored slowly and is a meal in itself. Serve on hot summer afternoons, and serve chilled! MAKES 1 TALL GLASS

1 pint plain yogurt
1 whole mango, peeled and sliced off the pit
2 tablespoons sugar
1 teaspoon cardamom powder, plus more for serving
A couple of ice cubes

Blend all of the ingredients in a blender until smooth and frothy. Sprinkle a little cardamom on the top.

fresh fruit tart

DIANA RABAIOLI

Diana Rabaioli and Ron Cavallo have been running Soigne for the past fifteen years. Soigne simply means something very special, hence a specialty shop. The demand for specialty items on the Island has risen dramatically over the years along with the population. To maintain high quality during the influx of crowds in the heat of the season, Diana must reserve her time for residents and locals. It's only in the dead of winter that a tourist can get one of her specialty desserts. This particular recipe is for a special local.

This may seem like far too much trouble, but the components can all be made a day or two ahead and then assembled on the day you'd like to serve it. Have fun with this one. Use whatever fruits you like on top of the tart and let your artistic juices flow into your design! MAKES 1 TART

Piecrust dough (see recipe on page 234)
2 ounces semisweet chocolate
1 cup plus 4 tablespoons heavy cream
6 tablespoons butter
⅓ cup sugar
1 tablespoon cornstarch
4 egg yolks
1 tablespoon vanilla extract
3 nectarines, sliced thin
2 kiwis, peeled and sliced
2 pints mixed berries (strawberries, raspberries, blueberries, blackberries—whatever looks best at the market)
½ cup apricot jam
1 tablespoon water

Heat the oven to 425 degrees.

Roll out your dough to ⅛ inch thick and line a 10-inch tart pan with a removable bottom. Prick dough all over with the tines of a fork. Line the pastry with foil, pressing firmly into the pastry. Bake for 10 minutes. Turn heat down to 350 degrees and continue to bake for 5 minutes more. Remove the foil and bake approximately 8 minutes more, or until the crust is golden brown. Remove from the oven and let cool.

Put the chocolate and 4 tablespoons of the heavy cream in a glass bowl and microwave for 1 minute. Remove and stir well, making sure all the chocolate is melted. Spread over the bottom of the pastry shell and chill.

Cook the butter, sugar, and cornstarch in a heavy 2-quart saucepan over medium-high heat. Stir constantly with a wooden spoon until the mixture thickens and boils. Boil for 1 minute.

Beat the egg yolks in a small glass bowl, then stir in a small amount of the hot sugar mixture. Slowly add the eggs to the mixture in the saucepan, stirring rapidly to avoid lumps. Cook over low heat, stirring constantly until the mixture coats the back of a wooden spoon, about 1 minute. Remove from the heat and stir in the vanilla. Cover and refrigerate until very cold, at least 3 hours.

When the egg mixture has chilled, whip 1 cup of heavy cream until it forms stiff peaks. Fold in the cold egg mixture and fill the pastry shell. Arrange the sliced nectarines in circles over the top of the tart. Top those with sliced kiwis and berries. Put the jam with the water in a glass bowl and microwave about 1 minute until melted. Glaze all the fruits with the jam mixture, using a pastry brush.

Chill your completed tart and serve with sweetened whipped cream.

indian carrot dessert

FRANCESCA KELLY

We all know carrots will work in cake, but we rarely think of carrots as the main ingredient in a dessert. Indians do not share this inhibition. After spicy dishes of chiles and other hot delicacies, this carrot dessert dish is a refreshing, but filling, finale. Preparation is simple; the only ordeal is grating carrots, and a good groom (husband or child) is ideal for this task. SERVES 10

12 to 15 medium carrots, washed, peeled, and grated
¼ pound (1 stick) unsalted butter
1 cup milk
Handful of raisins
½ cup sugar (organic, evaporated cane juice is best)

Heat the grated carrots, to dry them out, in a frying pan over low heat for 10 minutes, stirring occasionally. Add the butter and fry them on high heat until pasty, about 5 minutes. Add the milk, raisins, and sugar and continue on low heat until carrots caramelize. This takes approximately 8 minutes more. Transfer to a serving bowl and serve warm, or refrigerate and serve chilled. It's so different and delicious, you'll find yourself making this dessert again.

NORTH SHORE
beach party

By the time August rolls around, the weather is so warm and the light so dreamy one can barely justify being indoors. The boys want to sleep in a tent, Gary wants to fish, and I want to sit on a rock and gaze at the constellations. What we do not want to do is have big parties that require lots of shopping, standing on line at the market, or cleaning house.

Dinner on the beach, in August, is as good as it gets. Everyone loves a beach party, and while it appears to require much effort, with potluck it's really quite simple. Our friends and neighbors Paul Schneider and Nina Bramhall have the summer beach cookout down to a science. Last year they invited the usual suspects: various members of Nina's family, their neighbors, friends, and friends' houseguests. The location was a magnificent stretch of sandy beach along the North Shore.

The process of setting up a beach party is as much fun as the party itself, and all helping hands are welcome. The anticipation of the good time to come was on the faces of those making the trek from the back of Paul's pickup to the chosen location. Armed with coolers, sawhorses, grills, and children, we worked up a sweat and appetite before the party began. Lugging stuff onto the beach has its rewards: a cool presupper dip in the blue-green sea. It took Paul all of five minutes to assemble the table, which required nothing more than a colorful cloth and a big bunch of flowers. Children were put to work gathering driftwood for the fire, a welcome task at any age. Keeping the children out of the dunes and tall grass was virtually impossible—the best spying on adults can be done from the higher ground. Checking for ticks postparty is a mandatory rule!

Tommy and Phoebe arrived with sleeping baby Lulu and homemade vanilla ice cream. Rose brought Daphne's legendary fried chicken, and GoGo and Dave came bearing a bowl of marinated crabs and giant sea scallops. Charlie, with no time to cook, brought his guitar (always an excellent contribution), and Gary arrived late, grinning from ear to ear, with a freshly caught bonito in hand.

Paul, who makes grilling seem effortless and has impeccable timing, oversaw the preparation and cooking of sea-soaked corn on the cob, clams, mussels, oysters, and anything and everything that might taste better grilled.

As a blissfully happy Gary thinly sliced his bonito and prepared a wasabi and ginger dipping sauce, we heard a shout from the ocean. Everett Bramhall, Nina's brother, was standing up in his small skiff, clutching the tail of a keeper striped bass. He too wore a smile as wide as the North Shore. Paul waded out to his boat, retrieved the fish, and twenty minutes later it was devoured by all. It doesn't get much fresher than that.

The early evening light faded and we witnessed the breathtaking motion of the glorious pink sun as it slipped to the sea. What was once the cook fire now lured us close and, with the comforts of a guitar, marshmallows, graham crackers, and chocolate, we pulled up a piece of the beach and settled in for the final moments of the day. Children found laps to bury themselves in; adults found they had no problem consuming too many s'mores. Food, fire, song, the sound of the waves lapping the shore, shooting stars . . . summer.

smoked bluefish pâté

TESS BRAMHALL

Summer isn't summer without a beach picnic, and a beach picnic isn't complete without this Vineyard classic. If you are lucky enough to have a fisherman in the family, then you can start by smoking your own fresh-caught bluefish (in and of itself another summer classic). Otherwise you can buy smoked bluefish from your local fish market and go from there. I originally found this recipe in a Nantucket cookbook, which called for a blender to make the pâté. I prefer to do the blending by hand, lightly mashing the ingredients together with a fork, for a coarser, less creamy result. Smoked bluefish pâté is great on crackers, French bread, or crudités and is never better than when eaten on the beach while watching the sun sink behind the Elizabeth Islands. SERVES 10

  6 ounces smoked bluefish
  6 ounces plain cream cheese, at room temperature
  1 medium red onion, very finely chopped
  2 tablespoons fresh lemon juice
  Salt and freshly ground black pepper, to taste

Combine all of the ingredients in a nonreactive bowl. Mash and flake the fish with fork tines, and the cream cheese as well. Mix until everything is well integrated but maintains some texture.

  Serve with extra-crisp crackers.

daphne's fried chicken

BILL STYRON

Daphne Lewis's fried chicken is truly of presidential status, consumed with relish on more than one occasion by Bill Clinton. Actually, I value his judgment less because he is (or was) president than because he is a good ol' boy from Arkansas who knows how to assess the greatness of fried chicken like Daphne's, with its sublime blend of crunchiness and subtle greasiness (first-class fried chicken must have a touch of greasiness). One evening chez Styron on Martha's Vineyard, Clinton couldn't get enough of Daphne's product. His appetite was scandalous. At one o'clock in the morning, passing through the kitchen on his way out, he grabbed a leftover thigh and breast and was last seen munching in a kind of delirium of pleasure.

SERVES 12

> 2 free-range chickens, cut for frying
> Juice of 1 lemon
> 4 tablespoons Old Bay seasoning
> 2 tablespoons lemon pepper
> 2 tablespoons minced garlic
> Vegetable oil, for frying
> 2 cups all-purpose flour
> 1 tablespoon paprika
> 2 tablespoons salt

Wash the chicken parts in hot water, then rinse in cold water. Pat dry with paper towels. Squeeze the lemon over the chicken parts and let sit for 5 minutes. Place the chicken parts in a bowl and season with the Old Bay, lemon pepper, and minced garlic. Cover and leave in the refrigerator anywhere from 1 hour to overnight (overnight is best).

Fill a heavy-bottomed skillet with 2 inches of oil and heat to 450 degrees. It is very important that the oil be hot enough.

Combine the flour, paprika, and salt in a paper bag and shake the chicken in it 5 or 6 pieces at a time.

Turn down the heat under the skillet, shake off some of the excess flour from the chicken, and place the chicken pieces in the skillet. Slowly heat the oil back up to 450 degrees.

Cook the chicken for 5 minutes on each side. Turn the pieces over again and cook each side for another 5 minutes, or until both sides are a medium golden brown. (When cooking a lot of chicken, change the oil if the pan looks muddy or dark.) Let the chicken dry on paper towels.

sashimi bonito
with wasabi-ginger
dipping sauce

GARY STUBER

As I contemplated what I might provide for this beach potluck gathering, I envisioned the reaction of friends sampling a finely sashimied, just-caught bonito in that all-pervading late-afternoon western light. As I seized upon the idea, my next unsettling thought was—great idea, but one that would require the inordinate pure luck factor.

As my expedition wore on, searching all the suspect and likely haunts, my vision of the instant rapture caused by savoring this rare delicacy started to blur. I started questioning my expectations as well as my own cosmology. If what I had always maintained about the fishing pursuit was true—that it's about the process, not the result—what the hell was I doing out here?

Beating homeward in a steep southwest chop and a steeper existential funk, I resolved to try one more last-ditch not-so-secret spot. Cutting the engine as I arrived at the south end of the bar, I found that all was too quiet. Not a bird, not a ripple, nothing. Perhaps there was hope of finding a few fillets at one of the Menemsha fish markets. The ultimate disgrace. They always ask, "Did you catch this?" When I can answer in the affirmative the enjoyment quotient increases. If I say, "I went fishing but had to purchase this at the fish market," disappointment is palpable.

Peripherally I see a splash fifty yards away and a solitary bird circling it. I start the motor and am there in heavy heartbeats. I make one cast and in several cranks I am on! Reality has just taken a quantum leap. Now that's fishing! SERVES 6 TO 8

1 (5- to 8-pound) bonito

wasabi-ginger sauce
   ¼ cup toasted sesame oil
   ¼ cup virgin olive oil
   ½ cup Russian River Chardonnay
   ½ teaspoon finely grated fresh ginger

4 tablespoons tamari sauce
2 tablespoons mirin
2 tablespoons wasabi powder
Pickled ginger and additional prepared wasabi, for garnish

Fillet the fish in the traditional manner: Cut the fillet in half lengthwise along the obvious lateral bone line. Remove any bones and cut away any dark red meat. With half of the fillet on the cutting board, tail section to the left, start cutting slices from the right. Angle your knife at about 30 degrees and cut ½-inch-thick slices. Cut down to the skin, then turn the knife horizontally along skin to separate the flesh from the skin.

To make the sauce, whisk together the sauce ingredients and pour into a small dipping bowl. Serve on the sashimi cutting board with the small bowl of sauce, pickled ginger, and a ball of prepared wasabi paste.

WARNING: This delicacy has a lugubrious effect on even the most inhibited diners. There is only one catch to this recipe and that is catching the bonito.

orecchiette *with* broccoli rabe

RICKY VIDER

What caught my eye originally about this recipe was that two of my favorite things were in it: roasted almonds and broccoli rabe. What makes it so successful is the gutsy combination of big flavors: hot peppers, slightly bitter broccoli rabe, salty almonds, and chewy orecchiette. But besides the taste, the best thing about this dish is its versatility. It's equally good served hot as the centerpiece of a winter dinner or at room temperature as a side dish at a summer picnic.

SERVES 4 AS A MAIN COURSE

the oil
2 cups olive oil
2 or 3 dried red hot peppers, finely chopped (if you can't find
   dried hot peppers, red pepper flakes will do)

1 large bunch (about 1½ pounds) broccoli rabe
1 pound orecchiette (farfalle and gemelli are fine substitutes)
2 cloves garlic, peeled and finely chopped
1 cup sliced almonds, roasted (see page 89)
Coarse salt
Freshly grated Parmesan cheese, for garnish

To make the hot pepper oil, combine the olive oil with the dried peppers or 1 tablespoon of red pepper flakes (use more if you prefer a hotter flavor) in a saucepan over medium-low heat. Simmer for 15 minutes, then let it cool. (This will keep for weeks.)

Bring a large pot of water to a boil. Add salt and the broccoli rabe. Cook for approximately 3 minutes, just to remove the raw "crunch." Drain and run under cold water. Lay out the cooled broccoli rabe on a cutting board. Cut off and discard the bottom ½ inch of the stem. Chop the rest into ¾-inch pieces.

Again, bring a large pot of water to a boil. Add the pasta and salt, stirring occasionally, and cook until al dente. Orecchiette takes longer than most pasta, 18 to 20 minutes.

Put 4 tablespoons of the hot pepper oil in a large frying pan over medium heat. Add the chopped garlic and cook for 30 seconds, until fragrant. Add the broccoli rabe and continue cooking for 3 to 4 minutes, until tender but still bright green. Add ½ teaspoon of the chopped red peppers, stir, and remove from the heat.

Toss the sautéed broccoli rabe with the orecchiette. Sprinkle the top with roasted almonds and sprinkle with coarse salt (I use ½ teaspoon). Serve warm or at room temperature, garnished with Parmesan cheese.

a thing *or* two about grilling

PAUL SCHNEIDER

"Fire on beach is good. Food cooked on fire is good. Food cooked on fire on beach is very good."

What more, really, needs to be said? The first sentence describes the single greatest leap forward in human history since the discovery of caves. The second is no doubt the most important culinary achievement since peeling bananas. And the third, the divine synthesis of the first two? Well, let's just admit right here and now that before the invention of the beach barbecue there wasn't much point in walking upright and having a big brain.

Every summer we have a routine. We take a couple of legless Weber grills down to the sea, prop them on rocks, pile them high with charcoal, and light them up. It's a sort of bring-your-own-protein party. And your own bottle, too. And maybe a salad if you're feeling particularly civic. Or a guitar. In addition to the fire and the table (plywood on a pair of sawhorses), we supply the corn on the cob (which gets thrown on the grill, husks and all, after a soak in a bucket of seawater), the paper plates, the trash can, and the salt and pepper.

Every summer the routine ends the same way. We pile one of the Webers with driftwood, which makes for a nice legal fire in these parts. We roast marshmallows. We say, "Next summer, we'll do this far more often."

How to succeed:

1. **Don't be parsimonious with your charcoal.** People invariably arrive late with strange things they wish to grill and it's not fun to have to tell them the fire's died out. On a similar note, if you have more than one grill light them 20 minutes or so apart.

2. **Do your best to let other people grill their own contributions;** do your best to politely keep them from overgrilling anything that comes from the sea.

3. **Bring extra flipping, turning, serving, eating, and bottle-opening utensils.**

4. **Don't bring any flipping, turning, serving, eating, or bottle-opening utensils** that you would be heartbroken to lose in the sand.

5. **Bring a fillet knife and a jar of mayonnaise** in case somebody pulls a fish out of the sea and wants to slather it up and throw it on the grill. (If mayo is just a bit too Neanderthal for you, a little cold-pressed, extra-virgin, small-batch, numbered-bottle olive oil will do almost as well.)

6. **Flashlights, citronella candles, and kerosene lanterns** are always welcome, as are extra sweatshirts, beach towels, bug spray, and trash bags.

7. **Make a point of going back early the next morning** to check for any stray trash.

bivalves *à la* gronk

PAUL SCHNEIDER

1. Put shellfish—clams, oysters, mussels—on a hot grill.

2. Wait like a predator until they open.

3. Remove immediately and serve on a sand-free surface.

4. Eat immediately with sand-free fingers.

5. Wash fingers in ocean.

striper *on the* grill

EVERETT BRAMHALL

Don't go to a beach picnic without a fishing rod, especially if it's dusk in July or August. Should you be lucky enough to land a keeper bass—or, for that matter, a bluefish or even a bonito— you'll be the hero of the evening. I actually caught this striper from my boat on the way to this party, but I won't say where.

There's nothing better than the unadulterated taste of fresh fish, so all I recommend doing once it's filleted is to spread a light coating of Hellmann's mayonnaise on both sides, sprinkle it with freshly ground pepper, and throw it on the grill. Cooking time depends on the thickness of the fillets, but generally 5 minutes per side should do the job. Better yet, as soon as a knife will easily pass through the meat, it's ready to eat.

Of course, if the fish don't show up, you may want to have a bag of chips as a fallback.

sea scallops *and*
soft-shell crabs

GOGO FERGUSON

I love to eat! I love very fresh and simple recipes. Therefore, the soft-shells were cleaned and tossed in olive and sesame oils with salt and freshly ground pepper. The large sea scallops had just arrived at the market and were marinated in similar oils and very quickly grilled on hot coals. Soft-shell crabs are reasonably priced and such a delicacy when cooked on a grill. We are so lucky on the Vineyard to have such a bountiful harvest from our shores and our farms. SERVES 6

1 pound extra-large sea scallops
6 soft-shell crabs
½ cup sesame oil
½ cup olive oil
Salt and freshly ground black pepper

Marinate the scallops and crabs in the oils and salt and pepper to taste 2 hours ahead of time.

Heat a grill at the beach and cook your scallops and crabs until just charred and tender, 2 to 5 minutes. Transfer to a platter or directly to waiting dinner plates.

grilled shrimp

PAUL SCHNEIDER

My not-so-secret secret to grilled shrimp is to cook them over a hot fire for a very short time. Like fish, they keep cooking after you've taken them off, so the minute I think they may be done I take them off, knowing that by the time people eat them they certainly will be. This is even more true with an acidic marinade like the lime and cilantro one I used, which if left to its own devices for long enough would "cook" the shrimp into a nice ceviche with no fire at all. I use medium-large, unpeeled shrimp and cook them on short bamboo skewers, which make for easy serving, and don't need to be brought home and washed up at the end of the feast.

SERVES 8 TO 10

the marinade
   ½ cup olive oil
   1 cup fresh lime juice
   ¼ cup tamari sauce
   1 healthy handful cilantro
   2 peeled garlic cloves
   2 teaspoons brown sugar
   1 tablespoon freshly ground black pepper

   3 pounds medium shrimp

Put all the marinade ingredients into a blender. Blend well and pour over the shrimp in a large bowl. Cover and refrigerate for 1 to 3 hours, stirring occasionally.

Soak the wooden skewers for an hour in a tray of water. It keeps them from burning on the grill.

Thread the shrimp on wooden skewers, put the skewers in a resealable plastic bag, and head for the beach.

summer slaw

PATRIE GRACE

SERVES 8

1 small red cabbage, halved, cored, and sliced thin
1 small green or Savoy cabbage, halved, cored, and sliced thin
3 carrots, scrubbed and grated
3 green tomatoes, cut into small wedges
4 tablespoons mayonnaise
1 tablespoon balsamic vinegar
3 sprigs fresh thyme, chopped
1 tablespoon celery seed
1 tablespoon dill weed
6 chive flowers, broken into florets (optional)

Toss all the vegetables together in a large nonreactive salad bowl. Mix the mayonnaise, vinegar, herbs, and flowers, if using, in a separate bowl. Add the mayonnaise mixture to the vegetables. Toss well. Refrigerate at least 4 hours prior to serving. This slaw gets better the longer it sits.

butterscotch brownies

NINA BRAMHALL

I've been making these brownies since I was little. They were my family's favorite for two simple reasons: none of us (except my mom) appreciated the taste of chocolate yet, and they were the easiest thing in the world to make. Many years later, we've all realized what we were missing in the chocolate department, but we still whip these up whenever we need something we know everyone will love. They have gone to beach picnics, bake sales, dinner parties, class trips, and family gatherings for years, and I have never had any to take home. Which is a real shame, because they're always better the next day. MAKES 20 BROWNIES

 1 cup (2 sticks) unsalted butter
 2 cups (well-packed) light brown sugar
 2 large eggs, beaten
 1½ cups all-purpose flour
 2 teaspoons baking powder
 1 teaspoon salt
 1 teaspoon vanilla extract
 ¾ cup coarsely chopped walnuts (optional)

Heat the oven to 350 degrees and butter an 8×10-inch baking pan.

 Melt the butter in a medium saucepan over low heat. Remove from heat and add the sugar. Combine well. Let the mixture cool to room temperature, then transfer to a large mixing bowl. Add the eggs, mixing while adding.

 Sift the flour, baking powder, and salt into a bowl. Slowly add the dry ingredients to the wet, stirring while adding. When the wet and dry mixtures are well combined stir in the vanilla and the walnuts, if using.

 Scrape the batter into the pan. Bake the brownies for 35 to 45 minutes, or until a knife comes out clean. Remove from the oven and let the brownies cool for about 20 minutes before cutting. Serve them right out of the pan or arrange on a platter.

peach-blueberry cobbler

BETTINA THOMPSON STERN

Ripe summer fruits can be paired (or multiplied) in countless combinations. You can change this recipe to satisfy your favorite matchings or to include what happens to be in your pantry. This particular combination is a big hit with my three boys.

SERVES 8 TO 10

the filling
10 medium sweet, juicy peaches, cut into 1-inch pieces (about 10 cups)
3 cups blueberries
¼ cup sugar
1 teaspoon grated lemon zest
2 tablespoons all-purpose flour

the dough
½ cup sliced almonds, roasted (see page 89)
1½ cups all-purpose flour
5 tablespoons sugar
1½ teaspoons baking powder
1 teaspoon baking soda
½ teaspoon salt
6 tablespoons unsalted butter, cut into pieces and chilled
¾ cup heavy cream
1 large egg
1 teaspoon vanilla extract
½ teaspoon almond extract

the topping (optional)
2 tablespoons sliced almonds
1 tablespoon sugar

Heat the oven to 400 degrees. Butter and flour a 3-quart baking dish.

To make the filling, combine the peaches, blueberries, sugar, lemon zest, and flour in a large mixing bowl. Mix well. Place in the baking dish. Bake until the fruits are hot and bubbly, 20 to 30 minutes.

To make the dough, put the roasted almonds in a food processor and process until they are finely ground. Combine the flour, sugar, baking powder, baking soda, and salt with the ground almonds in a mixing bowl. Cut in the butter (using two knives or your fingers) until it is well mixed and crumbly. Whisk the cream, egg, and vanilla and almond extracts together in a separate small mixing bowl until well blended. Pour the cream mixture into the flour mixture and mix well with a wooden spoon (or your hands). The dough will be sticky.

When the fruits have cooked, remove the dish from the oven. Leave the oven on. Use an ice cream scoop to drop the dough evenly over the top of the hot fruit.

To make the optional topping, combine the almonds and sugar and sprinkle over the top of the cobbler.

Return the cobbler to the oven and bake until it is golden brown and the dough is cooked through, 15 to 20 minutes. Let it cool for half an hour before serving. I like it best served warm with vanilla ice cream.

autumn
POTLUCKS

FULL
moon

"There's a full moon on its way and it's coming on Friday the thirteenth. Let's have a party. Let's have a poetry potluck and everyone can bring food and a poem!" Carly loves a reason to socialize, and what better excuse could there possibly be than an October Hunter's Moon?

The invitation was simple: bring a dish that would go well with an autumn bisque and write a poem. *"Write a poem?"* came the horrified response of some of the nonpoet guests. The directions were clarified: write a poem, read a poem, sing a song, paint a painting, whistle a tune about the moon. Not only were our culinary skills being tested, but our creative ones as well.

Carly's gazebo sits on a hill overlooking a tranquil lily pond. From every angle one can see the sheep, donkeys, and horses that freely roam the fields. Guests arrived and we took our seats, hot toddies in our hands and blankets on our laps.

Margot, always the artist, brought a baked brie, the phases of the moon depicted elegantly on top. Patrick brought and presented to each of us a hand-rolled beeswax moon candle. Zack and Phyllis, just back from the mainland, brought a tray of exotic cheeses from their favorite shop, Formaggio Kitchen, in Cambridge. Our energy rose with the incoming tide, and warmed by our toddies and camaraderie, we began the first phase of the evening. Singers sang, musicians played, and writers and nonwriters read words close to their hearts.

I contributed a haiku by author Richard Wright. As I recited Wright's words about wild geese in the fall, a honking flock of geese flew directly over the gazebo and headed straight for the center of the gigantic rising orange moon.

Carly led us in a soulful rendition of "Moon River," followed by "Moon Dance," and "Paper Moon," as we crossed the stream and walked up the hill to our harvest dinner inside her house. Jaime's rosemary roasted chicken, Gary's basil and garlic mashed potatoes, Norman's codfish cakes, and Charlie's blue Hubbard squash pie were waiting.

We gravitated toward the crackle of the fire with bowls of soup and plates of steaming food. For a while there was silence and then the sound of Livingston Taylor at the piano filled the room.

We tried to remember the full moon names for each month according to the Algonquins. Sap Moon, Spearfish Moon, Harvest Moon, Planting Moon, Beaver Moon.... We could not recall them all, but we knew for certain that we would need to honor each one with a full moon poetry potluck.

autumn bisque

JAIME HAMLIN

This is the perfect soup for a cool fall evening, one that uses all of the bounty of the season: squash, apples, leeks, and cider. I've often served this in small hollowed-out pumpkins for a special dinner. SERVES 6

the soup
   3 pounds butternut squash, peeled and cut into 1-inch cubes
   3 leeks (white and light green parts), washed and sliced
   3 apples, cored, peeled, and cut into chunks
   4 tablespoons unsalted butter
   1 tablespoon vegetable oil
   1 tablespoon curry powder
   6 cups chicken stock
   1½ cups apple cider (not juice)
   ½ cup heavy cream
   Salt

the croutons
   ½ cup olive oil
   ¼ teaspoon paprika
   ¼ teaspoon salt
   1 clove garlic, minced
   1½ cups cubed French bread, crusts removed

   1 cup grated Asiago cheese

To make the soup, sauté the squash, leeks, and apples in the butter and vegetable oil in a skillet over medium heat. Cook until the leeks and apples begin to soften, about 5 minutes. Add the curry powder and sauté a minute or so more.

Pour in the chicken stock and the cider and bring to a boil. Then simmer over low heat for about 30 minutes. The squash should be very soft. Transfer in batches to the food processor and process until smooth. Return the bisque to the pot, stir in the cream, add salt to taste, and reheat.

Meanwhile, to make the croutons, heat the oven to 400 degrees and make the croutons. Combine the olive oil, paprika, salt, and garlic in a mixing bowl. Add the bread and toss. Place the bread cubes on a baking sheet and bake for 5 to 7 minutes, or until firm and golden.

Ladle the hot soup into bowls. Top with croutons and grated cheese.

baked brie

MARGOT DATZ

SERVES 15

1 package Pepperidge Farm puff-pastry sheets, thawed
Flour, for dusting board
1 (6-inch) wheel of brie, rind on
½ cup quality chutney, excess liquid drained so it is thick, not runny
½ cup fresh cranberries
½ cup milk, for sealing and glazing
Dried cranberries for garnish (optional)

Heat the oven to 400 degrees.

Roll out one pastry sheet on a floured board, large enough to wrap around the brie. Place the brie in the center of the pastry. Spread the brie with the chutney and then cover with the cranberries. Fold up the edges of the pastry like a little drawstring purse, trimming any excess, so that the cheese is completely encased except for the very top center.

Roll out the second pastry sheet, but not as thin. Cut out a shape to cover the top of the brie (a circle, a heart, a chubby star, a scallop shell, a leaf—just use your imagination).

Use a pastry brush to brush the encased cheese with the milk. This functions as a sealant. Lay the cutout top onto the encased cheese and press the circumference of the top down to perfectly seal the cheese in. This is very important—any leak in the pastry allows the melted cheese to escape in an oozy mess.

Brush the top with milk to glaze it as well. You may decorate your top with additional little cutouts to make it as fancy as you wish.

Place the cheese on a baking sheet with edges (just in case there is a leak) and bake until the pastry is puffy and golden, about 10 minutes.

Slide carefully off the pan (you may need a spatula, but don't puncture it!) and onto a platter. Surround it with dried cranberries, if desired. Let the cheese rest a bit. Accompany with husky crackers, lots of butter knives for spreading, and perhaps a small crock of honey mustard.

norman's indian hill codfish cakes

NORMAN HALL

This recipe comes from a little country in South America called Suriname. My mother was born there, and her mother handed the recipe down to her. She turned me on to these delectable little cakes as a kid. I picked up a few additional secrets during my eleven years living in Holland, where many of my relatives from Suriname reside. Of course, we are not able to get some of the ingredients in the United States, but I have listed the best substitutes I could think of. However, if you want to try them with the most delicious hot sauce "sambal," called Madam Jeanette Hotpepper, pay a visit to a "togo" during your next visit to Amsterdam or, better yet, visit Suriname.

A togo is a specialty market in Holland that sells foods native to Suriname.

SERVES 8 TO 10

3 pounds codfish (dried or fresh)
12 medium potatoes (Yukon gold)
2 sweet onions, finely chopped
1 cup chopped flat-leaf parsley
5 large eggs, beaten
Cayenne pepper to taste
Freshly ground black pepper
Fine Italian bread crumbs
Oil, for frying
For serving (optional)
   Wheatsworth crackers
   Chow-chow
   Dijon mustard
   Hot sauce

If you are using dried cod, cover it with cold water and soak for 24 hours in the refrigerator, changing the water at least twice. If you are using fresh cod, cover it with cold water, add 2 tablespoons coarse salt, and soak it overnight. Drain either before proceeding.

Boil the potatoes and onions for approximately 10 to 12 minutes in a large pot. Add the cod and continue cooking until potatoes are done. Drain well and transfer to a large mixing bowl. Mash with a potato masher until well combined. Add the parsley, eggs, and cayenne and black pepper to taste (start with ¼ teaspoon each).

Shape into cakes 2 to 3 inches in diameter. Put the bread crumbs in a bowl, dip the cod cakes in the crumbs, and fry in oil until golden brown. Serve between crackers with chow-chow, Dijon mustard, your favorite hot sauce, or just as they are.

herb *and* garlic roasted chicken

JAIME HAMLIN

There is nothing more delicious on a crisp fall evening than a savory rosemary-scented chicken. This recipe is a particular favorite of mine. The lemony roasted garlic sauce is divine. It's a great dish to bring to potluck suppers because this chicken is delicious at room temperature. Just be sure the sauce is hot! SERVES 6

1 (4-pound) roasting chicken
1 small onion
½ lemon
2 bunches fresh rosemary
1 bunch fresh thyme
¼ cup olive oil
Salt and freshly ground black pepper
20 cloves garlic, peeled
1 cup chicken stock
½ cup heavy cream
Juice of 1 lemon

Heat the oven to 425 degrees.

Put the chicken in a roasting pan and stuff it with the onion, lemon half, one bunch of rosemary, and half the thyme. Drizzle the olive oil over the chicken and season it with lots of salt and pepper.

Roast the chicken in the oven for about 30 minutes, then add the garlic cloves to the roasting pan. Stir the garlic in the pan juices and season them with salt. Continue to roast for another half hour or so, until the chicken is done (to check, pierce the chicken near the leg to see if the juices run clear). Remove the chicken to a cutting board.

Put the roasting pan on the top of the stove over medium-high heat. Remove all of the herbs. Use a wire whisk to mash up the garlic with the pan juices. Add the chicken stock, cream, and lemon juice. Whisk everything together and let the sauce reduce, stirring occasionally, for 4 to 5 minutes. You can strain this into a sauceboat or serve it with all the crispy bits in it!

Put the chicken on a serving platter and surround it with the remaining herbs.

basil, cream, *and* garlic mashed potatoes

"pass the mashed"

GARY STUBER

I grew up watching Mom make mashed potatoes. When I was old enough to assist her, around five or six, she would push a wooden milk crate up to the stove so that I could mash while she poured the milk and added the butter. We had a basement full of milk and butter, given my dad's job at a local dairy. Our ancient noisy refrigerator at the bottom of the stairs was chock-full of glistening bottles of milk and cream, rows of chunky butter, sour cream and cheese, and endless cartons of eggs. Over the years I have added my own ingredients to Mom's mashed potatoes. It remains the best comfort food I know, especially since my own six-year-old boys are now mashing at my side. I love to hear them say, "Dad, pass the mashed." SERVES 10 TO 12

12 medium Yukon gold potatoes, scrubbed
1 large bunch fresh basil, stems discarded
8 cloves garlic, peeled
2 to 3 cups whole milk
4 tablespoons unsalted butter
Salt and freshly ground black pepper

Quarter the potatoes and put them in a large stockpot. Cover them with water. Add ½ teaspoon of salt. Bring the potatoes to a rolling boil, turn the heat down to medium, and cook the potatoes until a fork will go through a piece effortlessly. Drain the potatoes. After they have cooled a bit, remove the skins.

Combine about 2 handfuls of basil leaves, the garlic, and 1 cup milk in a blender. Puree. Return the potatoes to the stockpot over low heat. Add the milk mixture slowly while simultaneously mashing vigorously. Add the butter and more milk as you mash (you will be pleasantly surprised by how much your heart rate increases). Temper the consistency by the amount of liquid you add. Food should have some texture so don't worry about it being somewhat lumpy. Those aren't really lumps, they're potatoes.

Taste for salt and pepper. Serve hot, in a huge bowl garnished with fresh basil.

fall greens sauté

PATRIE GRACE

I love greens. I find combining many of any season's freshest greens into one simple sauté gives more variety for a potluck gathering than any one green by itself.

SERVES 6 TO 8

1 pound broccoli rabe
1 pound Swiss chard
1 pound radicchio
1 pound kale
1 pound spinach
4 tablespoons unsalted butter (plus more if you want)
¼ cup olive oil
4 cloves garlic, minced
Kosher salt and freshly ground black pepper

Thoroughly wash and dry all greens. Discard any tough stems and chop the greens roughly.

Melt the butter with the olive oil in a large skillet over medium-low heat. Add the garlic and sauté for approximately 1 minute, until fragrant.

Add the broccoli rabe and sauté for 2 minutes more, then add the Swiss chard, radicchio, and kale. Sauté another 3 to 4 minutes. Last, add the spinach, salt and pepper to taste, and, if desired, more butter. Keep stirring while sautéing. Cook the greens until just tender, keeping their array of colors and tastes fresh.

Serve immediately.

down-island
caramel sauce

ROSE STYRON

What is the matter with Mary Jane?
She's humming a tune though her hunger's insane.
("It's lovely Potluckdom for dinner again!")
Nothing's the matter with Mary Jane.

Mary (Jane) Wallace, that is. She's driving up-island, tin cup in hand, having used a famous Wisconsin brand of flattery to persuade her southern pal Lazy Rosey to make quick down-island caramel sauce and bring it once again *as a contribution to the food fest. Mike will arrive later looking for Daphne's fried chicken. At dessert time, Mary-and-cup (Oliver Twist cadging drippings) will trail Rosey as she pours sauce over ice cream or brownies or gingerbread, by moonlight, firelight, the light of friendship extraordinaire, and song.*

Simplicity and portability are the watchwords of Vineyard potluck. Our neighbors' treats, new and old, are anticipated more joyously because none of us has to ruin an afternoon walk, tennis game, or daydream with the anxiety that precedes a dinner party at home. Also, after dark on a crowded beach, forbidden calories can be downed unnoticed. The feeling is distinctly great.

A rolling feast gathers no moss. SERVES 12

2 cups dark brown sugar, packed
½ cup light brown sugar, packed
½ cup heavy cream (or light cream, if you prefer a thinner sauce)
½ cup (1 stick) salted butter
A pinch or two of salt (I like two)

Combine both sugars in a heavy-bottomed pot with ½ cup water. Bring to a boil over medium-high heat, stirring until the sugars are dissolved. Reduce the heat to medium and stir in the cream, butter, and salt. Bring all of this back to a boil, then let simmer for a minute or so more. Remove from the heat and pour immediately into a serving pitcher.

blue hubbard squash pie

CHARLIE BRAUN

When I first started coming to Martha's Vineyard, in the late 1970s, it was to play music with my band, Zanzibar, at the Seaview Hotel. From the very first gig I was completely taken by the kind, engaging, and wild people I met. (I'm still very close with many of those first acquaintances.)

I've never stopped visiting friends on the Vineyard, and a recent opportunity to move here was a gift I just couldn't refuse. This time, however, I'm returning not only as a musician, but as a school psychologist and pie maker as well. I've sufficiently honed my craft with crust and filling to feel worthy of the quality of social life and eating on the Island (we're talking about a serious commitment to laid-back, interesting, hilarious, and conscientious connections to food and one another). Since off-island friends have learned that I have moved to the Vineyard, my favorite question has been "What do you think it's gonna be like to live there in the winter?" Hmmm . . . I just smile.

Blue Hubbard squash is really wonderful to use; it is identical to pumpkin in a number of ways, but it actually makes a more firm pie and tastes consistently as good as the best pie pumpkins. MAKES TWO 9-INCH PIES

1 blue Hubbard squash
3 cups milk (whole milk works well, or use 2¼ cups skim)
¾ cup brown sugar, packed
½ cup maple syrup (or white sugar)
5 large eggs, beaten
2 tablespoons molasses
1½ teaspoons vanilla extract
1 teaspoon salt
2 teaspoons ground cinnamon
1 teaspoon ground ginger
½ teaspoon grated nutmeg
¼ teaspoon ground cloves
2 (9-inch) piecrusts (see page 234)

Heat the oven to 425 degrees.

Cut the squash into chunks (you'll need a sharp knife and a strong arm). Scrape out the seeds, then steam the squash in a few inches of water in a stockpot, until soft. Scoop the squash out of its skin and whip with a heavy whisk until smooth. You'll need 4 cups of squash for 2 pies.

Combine the 4 cups of squash with the rest of the ingredients (except the piecrusts). Mix with a wooden spoon until smooth. Pour the filling into the piecrusts.

Bake at 425 degrees for 15 minutes, then turn down the oven to 350 degrees for another 35 to 40 minutes. When the pies are done, a sharp knife poked in the center will come out clean. Don't overcook, especially if you like your pies moist and pudding-like.

NOTE: If you'd like to garnish the pies, make a half batch of piecrust (page 234), roll it out and cut out leaf shapes. Mark veins with the back of a knife, and bake the pastry on a baking sheet at 350 degrees for about 30 minutes, until golden. Slip the leaves on the pie when you pull it out of the oven.

gar's
apple-strawberry
crisp

GARY STUBER

In the Berkshire Mountains in 1970, a barn full of maple syrup and a bumper crop of apples, coupled with a burning desire to make something other than gallons of apple sauce and scores of apple pies, led me to apple crisp.

It was flexible enough to allow for seasonal availability (whatever you had too much of), utilized vast amounts of my personal panacea, maple syrup, and could just as well be served for breakfast as for dessert.

Try any and all combinations of apples, strawberries, pears, rhubarb, raspberries, and peaches. SERVES 12

12 medium McIntosh apples
1 pound fresh strawberries
1 tablespoon ground cinnamon
¼ teaspoon ground ginger
½ cup apple cider
½ cup maple syrup

the topping
1 cup organic rolled oats
½ cup toasted wheat germ
½ cup whole wheat pastry flour
¼ teaspoon salt
½ cup maple syrup
⅓ cup canola oil
¼ cup apple cider
½ teaspoon ground cinnamon

Heat the oven to 350 degrees and butter a 9×13-inch baking dish.

Cut the apples into wedges, core, and cut them in half again—no need to peel. Remove the tops from the strawberries and cut them in half. Place the fruits in the buttered baking dish.

Mix the cinnamon, ginger, cider, and syrup in a bowl until well combined, then pour over the fruits.

To make the topping, combine all the ingredients. When they are well blended spoon the mixture over the fruits. Bake uncovered on the middle rack of your oven for 50 minutes. The top will be golden brown and the fruits soft and juicy. Serve warm, with vanilla ice cream.

LONG POINT
autumn
AFTERNOON

Long Point Wildlife Refuge consists of 633 acres of West Tisbury land, owned by the Trustees of Reservations, the oldest land trust in the nation. The landscape is unusual: a coastal sand plain created by outwash from the melting glacier. A magnificent beach surrounded by numerous coves and small ponds is a magnet for hikers. Several species of rare birds and other animals live among the endangered vegetation that grows on the sand plain, kept in check by periodic burning. Another amazing fact about Long Point is that it has a picnic table.

The picnic table (compliments of the trustees), positioned perfectly with a view of the pond and vast open fields, inspired this autumn lunch. There was a strong desire to squeeze in one more potluck gathering outdoors before the cold winds blew us inside. We phoned our friends, checked the forecast daily, and settled upon a Saturday in early November.

Eating outside is great. Eating outside on a table is even better. Getting food and plates to the table is not always that simple. I was told that, with advance permission, we could drive our picnic right up to the table and then return the cars to the lot. On the Thursday prior to the event I phoned the caretaker's house at the refuge—no answer. On Friday, I forgot to call back.

Saturday arrived and the weather was perfect. I loaded the car with green jadeite (my favorite picnic dishes), tablecloths, silverware, glasses, napkins, Gary's maple-pecan panoche, and Noah and Jules, fresh from soccer practice. We drove down the seemingly endless dirt road, which had far more potholes than I remembered.

I reached the entrance to Long Point and was immediately stopped by a chain hooked from one side of the road to the other. A large sign reading KEEP OUT—NO CARS BEYOND THIS POINT—WILDLIFE REFUGE stared me in the face. Okay. Plan B. I parked the car in the lot, went to the caretaker's house, and knocked on the door. No one home. Plan C. Walk everything in down the long path to the picnic table, think of it as excellent exercise, and hope everyone else arrives early enough to help.

The day was so gorgeous even the poison ivy along the way looked good enough for a bouquet. Seaside goldenrod covered the dunes, and sassafras and scrub oaks were ablaze with color.

Soon friends arrived and they too carried their baskets of food to the site. The table, set in fall colors, looked ever so inviting as it received platters of chèvre, sun-dried tomato, and asparagus wraps, caramelized onion tarts, baskets of walnut levain, and warm gingerbread with dried fig, apricot, and cherry compote. Nearby a small gas stove (also hiked in) warmed roasted chicken and wild rice chowder.

As we sat down to eat we might as well have been the only ones in the world, alone there by the edge of the sea. The children played at being pirates, searching for hidden treasures, ate candied apples, and smiled toothless grins. Fellini would have liked this scene.

Hours passed, and with bellies full and minds relaxed, we paraded back to civilization. The low, all-pervasive afternoon light cast long shadows reaching out to Tisbury Great Pond. We realized it was days like these that remind us why we live here.

steak, arugula, *and* parmesan wraps

MEGAN AND NATHAN WILSON

We thought about making roll-ups at home after having an incredible salmon club wrap from Johnny's Carryout in Vineyard Haven. They are simple to make and can accommodate innumerable variations, depending on what you happen to have in the refrigerator. Leftovers are good. We also like to make roll-ups when we go to the beach. Our beach mixture tends to consist of rice, steamed vegetables, and miso dressing. SERVES 8

3 porterhouse steaks, 1½ inches thick (about 2 pounds)
2 tablespoons Worcestershire sauce
2 tablespoons Dijon mustard
3 generous tablespoons black olive pesto
¾ cup mayonnaise
8 spinach, red pepper, or plain flour tortillas
8 cups loosely packed arugula
¾ pound Parmesan cheese, shaved in strips (using a peeler)
2 red bell peppers, seeded and cut into long strips
Salt and freshly ground black pepper

Prepare a grill or heat a stovetop grill pan over medium-high heat.

Rub the steaks with Worcestershire and mustard and then grill them about 3 minutes per side, or to your preferred doneness. Let sit for about 10 minutes, then slice into strips.

Mix the pesto and mayonnaise in a small mixing bowl and spread on the wraps. Layer each tortilla with a handful of arugula, a few strips of steak, Parmesan shavings to cover, and several red pepper strips. Salt and pepper to taste. Fold the bottom of the wrap over the filling, then roll left to right, leaving the top open. Leave whole or cut in half on the diagonal.

chèvre, sun-dried tomato, *and* asparagus wraps

MEGAN AND NATHAN WILSON

SERVES 8

2 bunches asparagus (or more, depending on size of bunch and thickness of spears—
   be generous)
8 spinach, red pepper, or plain flour tortillas
4 ounces chèvre (fresh goat cheese)
12 to 14 sun-dried tomatoes in oil, cut into long strips
6 ounces baby spinach
2 red bell peppers, seeded and cut into strips
Salt and freshly ground black pepper
8 marinated artichoke hearts, sliced (optional)
Toasted pine nuts (optional)

Steam the asparagus until just tender.

Spread each tortilla with goat cheese, then make layers of sun-dried tomato strips, spinach, red pepper strips, and asparagus spears. Add salt and pepper to taste. Optional additions are the sliced artichoke hearts or pine nuts, or both.

Fold the bottom of the wrap over the filling, then roll left over right, leaving the top open. Leave whole or cut in half on the diagonal.

roasted chicken *and* wild rice chowder

CHRISTIAN THORNTON

Christian Thornton, chef de cuisine at Atria restaurant in Edgartown, developed his love of food while growing up in San Francisco and spending his summers on the Great Lakes. He and his partner, Greer G. Boyle, met while working together at an organic Asian fusion restaurant in Washington, D.C. After visiting Greer's family vacation spot on Martha's Vineyard they decided to settle here and build their dream.

The recipe they carried to the picnic on that beautiful fall afternoon was a combination of flavors from all the places they had experienced, brought together in New England–style chowder. Whole grains and wild rice were a nod to Christian's summers in the Midwest, chicken was chosen simply as a healthy and delicious fall flavor, a joint belief in good and natural ingredients stemmed from their study of organics, and the chowder . . . well, that part is obvious.

The only lesson to realize after allowing yourself to make up your own recipes is that chowders, like a lot of foods, are subject to many variations and tastes. The only staple is love. SERVES 8 TO 10 AS A STARTER

1 pound boneless chicken breast
¼ pound bacon
2 medium onions
4 carrots
4 stalks celery
1 pound potatoes
2 tablespoons vegetable oil
6 cups chicken stock
6 sprigs fresh thyme, leaves picked
2 bay leaves
2 cups heavy cream
2 cups cooked wild rice
Salt and freshly ground black pepper
Grated zest of 1 lemon

Cut the chicken, bacon, and vegetables into about ¾-inch dice. Sauté the chicken and bacon in the oil over high heat in a heavy-duty pot, until browned. Add the onions, carrots, celery, and potatoes and continue to cook until the vegetables are tender, approximately 25 minutes.

Add the chicken stock, thyme, and bay leaves and simmer over low heat for 20 minutes. Stir in the cream and wild rice and cook to heat through. Add salt and pepper to taste.

Remove the bay leaves and serve in bowls. Garnish with lemon zest.

napa *and* cilantro salad *with* spicy peanuts

LAURA D. ROOSEVELT

When I moved to Martha's Vineyard from New York City, the only two things I missed were good Asian restaurants and takeout places that deliver. I can't solve the takeout problem, but I've learned to make sushi, Thai curries, Chinese stir-fry dishes, and lots of Indian vegetarian food. I've become my own Asian restaurant.

This dish has a Vietnamese feel to it. The apple cider—a secret ingredient I use often, especially as a replacement for some of the oil in salad dressings—serves both to cut the oil and to help counteract the bitterness of limes. SERVES 12

the dressing
   ⅓ cup toasted sesame oil
   ½ cup rice vinegar
   ¼ cup soy sauce
   ⅓ cup apple cider or juice
   Juice of 3 small limes
   ¼ cup sugar
   2 tablespoons minced fresh ginger
   1 teaspoon minced jalapeño pepper

the peanuts
   ¾ cup unsalted peanuts
   2 tablespoons Tabasco sauce
   1 tablespoon vegetable oil

the salad
   ½ head Napa cabbage, outer leaves removed, inner leaves washed, dried, and thinly
      sliced
   1 cup loosely packed cilantro leaves
   2 scallions, thinly sliced, including some green part
   3 large carrots, peeled and cut into thin strips
   4 red bell peppers, seeded, halved, and cut into thin strips

To make the dressing, whisk together the ingredients in a small bowl and set aside.

To make the peanuts, heat the oven to 350 degrees. Combine the peanuts, Tabasco, and vegetable oil in a bowl and mix well. Spread out on a small baking

sheet and bake until browned, about 20 minutes. Stir once with a spatula during the roasting. Let cool.

To make the salad, combine the salad ingredients and the peanuts in a large salad bowl. Pour on about half of the dressing, just enough to moisten it. (Save the other half for another time; it keeps well in the refrigerator.) Toss until well coated and serve.

peanut butter *and* jelly roll-ups

MOLEE B. LEWIS

My biggest concern with feeding my children is getting them to focus long enough to eat a healthy meal. There are always "superhero" distractions. I tell my three-year-old that Buzz Lightyear has to eat to get the energy he needs to save the universe. I try to make food fun to look at and fun to eat. As the saying goes, "It's all in the presentation" (especially for a three-year-old). MAKES 8

8 whole wheat tortillas
Creamy peanut butter
Raspberry jam
Fruit of the season, peeled and cut in child-size pieces (clementines are a favorite with kids)

Prepare the tortillas by spreading peanut butter and jelly on each one, then roll lightly. Serve whole. Another option, once you have rolled the tortilla, is to slice it into bite-size pieces so your kids can simply pop them into their mouths! Either way, garnish with fruit.

caramel apples

PATRIE GRACE

MAKES 12

12 tart apples
12 Popsicle sticks
1 cup (2 sticks) unsalted butter
2¼ cups brown sugar, packed
2 cups light cream
1 cup light corn syrup
1 teaspoon vanilla extract
1 cup chopped walnuts or peanuts (optional)

Butter a baking sheet.

Wash and dry the apples and remove the stems. Insert a wooden Popsicle stick (the wide ones hold up best) into the stem end of each apple. Place the apples on the baking sheet.

Melt the butter in a heavy 3-quart saucepan over low heat. Add the brown sugar, light cream, and corn syrup and mix well. Cook and stir over medium-high heat until the mixture boils. Clip the candy thermometer to the side of the saucepan. Reduce the heat to medium and continue to boil (but not too rapidly), stirring constantly until the thermometer registers 248 degrees. Remove from heat. Remove the candy thermometer and stir in the vanilla. One at a time, working quickly, dip each apple in the hot caramel. Turn to coat. Dip the bottom of the apples in walnuts or peanuts, if desired. Set back on the baking sheet. Chill before serving to set the caramel.

caramelized onion tart

ALICE BERLOW

This recipe evolved from Maggie's kitchen. She was my neighbor when I lived in the suburbs of Boston. Our friendship was founded when we had our first babies within a month of each other. We were both new moms feeling housewifely and homebound.

Maggie was a chef in her prechildbearing life. You could tell by how Maggie worked, what she made, and her improvisational cooking style that she was a pro. She knew how to mix, match, and feel her way around whatever ingredients she had on hand. She told fantastic food stories from restaurant life and introduced me to the writings of M.F.K Fisher. For that I will always be grateful.

When she cooked I used to sit on the threshold of her kitchen with our babies, well away from the action. With George Clinton funking out on the stereo we watched in awe as she took butcher knives to sides of beef, baked chocolate ganache cakes for our coffee klatches, and simmered broths from the bones of roasted chickens for the first comforting soups we fed to our yearlings. She was a whirlwind of creative cooking. It kept her sane and those around her well fed. She was my hero and still is. Cheers to you, Maggie, and thanks! SERVES 8 TO 10

1 package dry active yeast
½ cup tepid water (about 110 degrees)
¼ teaspoon sugar
¾ cup milk
3 cups all-purpose flour, plus extra for dusting work surface
1 cup whole wheat flour
1½ teaspoons salt
2 tablespoons olive oil

the topping
2 tablespoons olive oil, plus additional for brushing
2 to 4 large Vidalia onions, peeled and sliced (¼ inch thick or less)
1 tablespoon sugar
3 tablespoons Dijon mustard
2 tablespoons dried oregano
Salt and freshly ground black pepper
10 ounces mozzarella cheese, shredded
8 ounces kalamata olives, pitted

Mix the yeast, water, and sugar in a bowl, let it sit for 5 minutes, then stir in the milk.

Put the flours and salt in a food processor. Process in the yeast mixture slowly, then add the oil. Process until the dough forms a ball. The dough will be soft. Let it rest in the food processor for 5 minutes. Turn it onto a lightly floured work surface and knead for 3 minutes. Let it rest a couple of minutes and knead another minute to make a soft, smooth dough.

Allow the dough to rise for about 1½ hours in a large bowl covered with a warm, damp cloth. It will double in bulk.

Heat the oven to 400 degrees.

To make the topping, heat the oil in a large skillet over medium-low heat. Add the onions and cover, but stir frequently, checking that the heat is not too high. Add the sugar to help the onions caramelize. Keep heat on low. The onions are done when they are limp and a golden caramel color.

Roll the dough out to fit an 11×17-inch baking pan.

Brush the dough with olive oil. Use your fingers or a spatula to spread a thin layer of mustard. Season with 1 tablespoon of the oregano and salt and pepper. Place on the lower oven rack. Bake for 7 to 9 minutes, until springy. Cool about 45 minutes.

Heat the oven to 350 degrees.

Scatter the cheese over the cooled crust, then spread the onions over the cheese. Top with the olives and sprinkle with the remaining tablespoon of oregano. Bake on the middle rack for 5 to 6 minutes, until the cheese melts. Serve hot or at room temperature.

maple-pecan panoche

GARY STUBER

In upstate New York in 1969, maple sugaring took on a decidedly cultlike appeal. It's a mysterious, fiery process that yields a sweet, earthy elixir; one felt as if it should be illegal. All that was needed was the will, a strong back, a warm hat, and some basic equipment, readily purchased from some other devotee who no longer found it particularly profitable.

In late spring when the barn was packed with brown boxes full of quart jars with white lids, we used it on anything that seemed the better for it—in coffee, on morning cereal, over ice cream, in salad dressing, tomato sauce, even by the shot glass. That subtle, round maple flavor shining through made them all seem complete. After much alchemy, I finally cracked the code and came up with "pan-oakee" (as the locals called it). You need a large (about 12×16 inches) slab of marble to make this. SERVES 15 TO 20

> 1 gallon maple syrup
> 1 pound (4 sticks) unsalted butter
> 1 pound pecans

Heat the oven to 400 degrees.

Heat the maple syrup in a stockpot over low heat, clipping a candy thermometer to the side of the pot. Melt the butter (do not boil) in a saucepan. Toast the pecans on a cookie sheet in the oven until dark brown, 10 minutes maximum.

Turn the heat up to the maximum under the syrup. Make a tent over the pot with aluminum foil, leaving the thermometer exposed. Watch the thermometer carefully. Cook until the syrup reaches 240 degrees, then remove the pot from the heat.

Stir in the pecans and the melted butter. Continue to stir for 1 minute to develop sugar crystals. Stir gently 1 minute more. Overstirring will make the panoche more dense, like maple sugar.

Pour the mix out onto a cold marble slab. When the panoche is completely cooled (about 45 minutes) cut into 1-inch squares with a sharp knife and serve.

ali's surfin' gingerbread

ALICE BERLOW

For me a potluck is the perfect opportunity to take a chance. I surf the Web. Food-related websites are plentiful and varied. I have my favorites, but like a surfer, I'm not about to reveal where the good waves are; you've got to go and find them for yourself. And the next time you are invited to a potluck, forget your tattered recipe cards. Take a chance and try something new.

I paired this moist gingerbread with bourbon-spiked dried fruit compote for a luscious finale to the feast. Serve it with your favorite compote or surf for a new one on the Net. Here's a hint: Try the keyword "fig." SERVES 8

3 cups all-purpose flour
2 teaspoons baking soda
2 teaspoons ground ginger
1½ teaspoons ground cinnamon
½ teaspoon ground cloves
½ teaspoon freshly grated nutmeg
¼ teaspoon black pepper
½ teaspoon salt
1 cup (2 sticks) unsalted butter, melted and cooled slightly
1 cup light brown sugar, packed
1 cup molasses
2 large eggs
⅔ cup crystallized ginger, chopped
Whipped cream, for garnish

Heat the oven to 350 degrees and position the rack in the center of the oven. Generously butter and flour a 12-cup Bundt pan.

Sift the flour, baking soda, ground ginger, cinnamon, cloves, nutmeg, pepper, and salt into a medium bowl. Combine the melted butter and brown sugar in a large bowl. Beat until well blended. Gradually beat in the molasses, then the eggs. Add the dry ingredients and continue beating until well blended. Gradually beat in 1 cup hot water. Stir in the chopped crystallized ginger.

Transfer the batter to the pan. Bake about 55 minutes, until a tester inserted near the center of the cake comes out completely clean.

Turn cake out onto a rack and cool completely. The cake can be made 1 day ahead. Wrap it in plastic and let stand at room temperature until ready to serve.

To serve, cut into 8 wedges, place on plates, and spoon some compote alongside each wedge, if you've made it. Garnish with sweetened whipped cream.

winter
POTLUCKS

SEVEN
GATES
appetizer
FETE

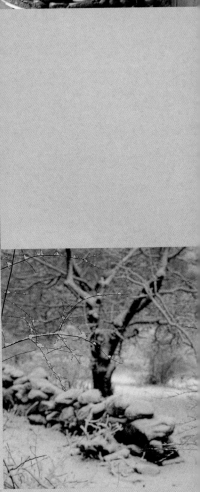

The faces one sees on the Vineyard in early December belong to people who live here year-round. Seasonal renters have long gone, and holiday visitors have yet to arrive. It is a time when one runs into friends at the gas station, post office, hardware store, or café. Questions often heard include, "Did you survive the summer?" or "Are things slowing down for you yet?"

Things don't slow down on the Vineyard off-season the way they once did. Most of the people I know are fully employed, busy with their jobs, families, and community work. December just means that they are busy in different ways from those of July. December means that they might make Bonnie's Monday night yoga class after all or clean out their mudroom or begin that 350-page novel they've been threatening to read. They might even take a ride all the way to Aquinnah, just to listen to some new tunes in the car and watch the winter wonderland pass by.

By December experimenting in the kitchen takes on new meaning. Talk is of braiding bread, Mexican spices, new toppings for popcorn. Recipe swapping is in the air.

Potlucks get people cooking in the winter. Feeling housebound by the occasional nor'easter, blizzard, or plain old gray day, one welcomes the opportunity to sit by the warmth of someone else's roaring fire and a change of fireplace scenery.

Early evening get-togethers guarantee at least the chance of getting to bed at a reasonable hour (we must be getting older) to replenish precious sleep lost during the hectic summer.

It was an early Sunday evening when twenty of us gathered for an appetizer potluck at Nina and Paul's house in the woods of West Tisbury. Those who arrived on time were able to appreciate the spectacular view of Naushon and Pasque Islands. The view, greatly enhanced by the absence of leaves on the trees, seemed five times as wide as in the summer, and keen eyes could trace the horizon from the Gay Head Light all the way to Woods Hole. Latecomers were treated to a star-studded sky and the twinkling lights of New Bedford, miles and miles away.

As usual, the bounty of the sea was well represented by Moshup mussels, baby stuffed quahogs, up-island oysters, seared tuna with wasabi aioli, cucumber and salmon rolls, and Miss Annie's smoked salmon tartar. For those feeling fished out there was plenty more to be tempted by, like pears on dark bread, crudités with spicy peanut sauce, caviar and tapenade dips, and a colorful green salad. I think everyone reached at least once for a juicy clementine from the overflowing bowl.

Happily, at the end of the evening, we picked up our empty platter, once laden with oysters, and set out for the drive home. As we negotiated our way along the winding dirt road we were startled by a buck leaping over the hood of our car. I can't remember a Sunday evening more satisfying—or more entertaining—than this.

cucumber *and* salmon rolls

JILANA ABRAMS

This is an hors d'oeuvre that I frequently serve with great success. I have experimented with many variations, among them sprinkling with sesame seeds instead of caviar. Other types of smoked fish can also be substituted. Thin sprays of scallion add an attractive accent. MAKES 20 ROLLS

1 English cucumber, peeled
10 slices smoked salmon
2 tablespoons wasabi powder
1 small jar pickled ginger
About 1 ounce black or red caviar, for garnish (optional)
Scallions, for garnish

Slice the cucumber with a cheese or vegetable slicer lengthwise, about ⅛ inch thick. Cut the cucumber and salmon slices into 4- to 5-inch lengths.

Mix the wasabi with 2 tablespoons water to make a paste in a small bowl. Spread a very thin layer of wasabi on each cucumber slice. Top this with the salmon.

Place a few slices of pickled ginger at one end of the cucumber. Roll and press firmly. Use toothpicks to secure your roll.

Serve on a platter with spirals facing upward. Sprinkle with the caviar and garnish with scallions—chopped or left whole.

up-island oysters *with* never-fail cocktail sauce

GARY STUBER

You will need about 6 oysters per serious shellfish consumer. Oysters are now widely available from far and wide, but I'd select those that are closest to home.

A word about opening these bivalves. You will need a shellfish knife and a coarse dish towel. Place the oyster on a cutting surface and hold it with a towel. Find the hinge and apply the point of the knife with ample pressure to insert the tip and, using it as a fulcrum, turn the handle clockwise a quarter turn as you move it to the left forcefully. Run the blade around the interior of the shell to free the oyster, being careful to spill as little of that precious liquid as possible. If done in one motion, with some style, this should yield several dozen nicely prepared oysters.

the sauce

- ½ cup organic tomato puree
- ¼ teaspoon fresh lemon juice
- 2 tablespoons dry white wine
- 1 dash chipotle hot sauce
- 1 tablespoon fresh grated horse-radish

- 2 to 2½ dozen oysters
- 1 lemon, sliced in wedges, for garnish

Whisk together the ingredients in a small mixing bowl. Pour the sauce into a small serving bowl and place it on a platter surrounded by oysters and freshly sliced lemon wedges. Watch them disappear.

classic italian bruschetta

JACI PEPPER

This is my interpretation of my husband John's family's bruschetta, a staple with drinks or even for breakfast, since the garlic wards off all evils (and keeps you healthy)! When I first arrived at their home in Italy, a fifteenth-century castello in Umbria, they were all in the kitchen collectively preparing the bruschetta and opening bottles of Chianti.

It's a cross-cultural standard—all you need to pull it off is some hearty bread, good-quality olive oil, and lots of garlic. Turn up the Vivaldi. SERVES 10 TO 12

2 loaves Italian, peasant, or sourdough bread
6 cloves garlic, peeled
½ to ¾ cup olive oil
1 bunch fresh basil, finely chopped
½ teaspoon sea salt

Heat the oven to 400 degrees.

Cut the bread into ¼-inch slices and toast them lightly in the oven. Take a peeled clove of garlic in your hand and firmly rub it back and forth over one side of the toast, as though it were sandpaper.

Whisk the olive oil with the basil and salt. Brush the toasts with the olive oil mixture on the garlic side. Serve these aromatic crisps warm.

tapenade dip

MARY ETHERINGTON AND CHRIS BURRELL

Mary Etherington and Chris Burrell are both artists and writers. Mary runs her own art gallery on the harbor in Vineyard Haven called Etherington Fine Art. She writes essays and travel stories. Chris, Mary's husband, is a writer for the Vineyard Gazette *and an illustrator who contributes to the* New York Times, Washington Post, *and* Boston Globe. SERVES 12 TO 16

½ cup kalamata olives, pitted
¼ cup Sicilian green olives, pitted
6 anchovy fillets
1 clove garlic
2 tablespoons capers
2 tablespoons tuna packed in oil, drained
1 tablespoon fresh lemon juice
¾ cup fresh basil leaves
½ cup cilantro
¼ cup extra-virgin olive oil
Salt and freshly ground black pepper

Combine the olives, anchovies, garlic, capers, tuna, lemon juice, basil, and cilantro in the bowl of a food processor fitted with a steel blade. Mix until it is a smooth paste. With the processor still on, begin to pour the olive oil in a fine stream to thicken the sauce. Taste it and adjust your seasonings.

Transfer the dip to a small serving bowl and refrigerate at least 1 hour. Serve the tapenade with fresh, seasonal vegetables. In the unlikely event that there is any left over, use the tapenade in your next batch of homemade tomato sauce for a zesty puttanesca!

caviar dip

MARY ETHERINGTON AND CHRIS BURRELL

SERVES 10 TO 12

3 ounces sour cream
6 ounces whipped cream cheese
1 tablespoon fresh lemon juice
1 teaspoon grated shallot
1½ tablespoons finely chopped fresh dill
A pinch of freshly ground black pepper
2 ounces black caviar or red salmon caviar

Blend the sour cream and cream cheese together in a medium mixing bowl. Fold in the lemon juice, shallot, dill, and pepper with a rubber or wooden spatula. Next, gently fold in the caviar. Refrigerate for at least 1 hour. Serve the chilled caviar dip with crispy crackers, toasted pitas, and fresh crudités.

crudités *with* spicy peanut dipping sauce

CLAUDIA LEE

When I bring hors d'oeuvre to a party I always consider two factors: the problem of being too busy running my two jewelry stores to have any cooking time, and wanting to bring a healthful plate of something I myself can eat.

If it's Sunday, I'll have time to make this spicy peanut dipping sauce with an array of raw or nearly raw assorted vegetables. Choose what's fresh and local; those will certainly be the sweetest. SERVES 20

the sauce
8 tablespoons natural peanut butter
8 tablespoons soy sauce
8 tablespoons mayonnaise
4 tablespoons dark brown sugar
6 to 8 cloves garlic, finely chopped
4 tablespoons fresh lemon juice
2 teaspoons red pepper flakes

the veggies
Red, yellow, and orange bell peppers
Cucumbers
Summer squash
Asparagus, very lightly steamed
Snap peas
Scallions
Broccoli florets
Cherry tomatoes

To make the sauce, whisk all of the sauce ingredients vigorously in a small mixing bowl. If your mixture seems too thick to be dippable add some water a tablespoon at a time. Cover with plastic wrap and refrigerate at least 30 minutes. The dipping sauce can be made up to 2 days ahead.

Arrange your fresh vegetables on a serving platter, leaving room in the center or off to one side for the dipping bowl. Pour the chilled sauce into a dipping bowl and garnish with a few fresh flowers or sprigs of garden herbs.

miss annie's smoked salmon tartar

TONI RUSSCOL COHEN

My mother always told me that my grandmother was really a Russian princess, stolen by the Gypsies from her father the Czar. That was why I shouldn't sass her! This is one version of her favorite hors d'oeuvre. SERVES 10

8 ounces smoked salmon, coarsely chopped
1 medium red onion, finely chopped
2 tablespoons capers
Juice of 1 lemon
2 tablespoons finely chopped chives
1 baguette, thinly sliced
½ cup garlic olive oil
1 small jar caper berries
Kalamata olives, pitted and coarsely chopped, for garnish
1 lemon, sliced, for garnish

Mix the salmon, onion, capers, lemon juice, and chives together in a medium mixing bowl.

Lightly toast the baguette slices under your broiler or in a toaster oven. With a pastry brush spread a thin coating of the garlic oil on the toasts. Take a teaspoonful (or your fingers work well) of the salmon mixture and mound it on top of the toasts. Serve on a platter garnished with caper berries, kalamata olives, and lemon slices.

grazing greens salad

LOUISE SWEET

Living on the Vineyard with a couple of teenage boys, a husband, and a flourishing flower business demands that I be able to pull things together at the drop of a hat more times in a year than I care (or have time) to count! Not only that, but by the very nature of my business, friends and family have come to expect that they can count on me to bring something that looks as good as it tastes. In my whirlwind Island existence I have perfected a few things that actually require no cooking, just gathering and presentation. I have been asked time and again to contribute my Grazing Greens Salad that looks so pretty and tastes so good and is always a fresh and delicious accompaniment to any feast. I began to make it a finger salad so that it is easier to gather in your fingers and get a good crunch of tostini (mini-toasts), a soft cheese, and a bit of greens or fruit, with or without a fork. Your guests can dip into a bit of cheese with tostini or help themselves to a plateful of greens. It's always fun to alter the ingredients as needed by season or availability, and it never fails to look colorful and inviting. Yum. SERVES 15

6 ounces baby spinach
8 ounces mesclun mix
1 bunch watercress
1 bunch arugula
1 bunch cilantro
2 clementines, peeled and sectioned
½ pound feta cheese
4 ounces pine nuts
½ pomegranate, peeled and seeded
1 round fromage de chèvre (fresh goat cheese)
3 ounces Italian tostini
½ pint raspberries
Balsamic vinegar

The joy of this beautiful salad is that you need only to toss all but the last 4 ingredients in your favorite large bowl. In the center put the round of fromage de chèvre, surround the chèvre with the tostini, and garnish with raspberries. Sprinkle just a bit of balsamic vinegar on right before serving.

stuffed baby quahogs

PEGGY SCHWIER

Most potluck meals I go to are often cast parties after one of our choreographer's workshops or community chorus concerts. And we haven't eaten for hours! I try to think of something substantial that I might crave and make a bite-size version of it.

I usually think seafood first, head out to the garden for the embellishments, and see where I end up. SERVES 15 TO 20

2 tablespoons unsalted butter
2 tablespoons olive oil
3 scallions, thinly sliced
¼ red bell pepper, cored and diced
¼ yellow bell pepper, cored and diced
2 cloves garlic, minced
2 teaspoons finely chopped fresh thyme
1 teaspoon finely chopped fresh sage
8 thin slices of peasant bread (I use Black Dog Bakery bread), toasted and cut into tiny cubes for stuffing)
30 littleneck clams, shucked over a bowl to reserve liquid, saving the shells
2 tablespoons finely chopped flat-leaf parsley
2 tablespoons fresh lemon juice
Coarse salt and freshly ground black pepper
2 tablespoons hot paprika, for garnish

Heat the oven to 375 degrees.

Melt the butter in a frying pan. As it melts add the olive oil, then sauté the scallions, peppers, and garlic for about 3 minutes. Remove the pan from the heat. Add the thyme, sage, and bread crumbs. Toss this mixture well, coating the bread cubes.

Chop the littleneck clams. (If you like your clams somewhat invisible chop them finely; I like mine a little coarser so the clams are still identifiable.) Add these to the bread crumb mixture. Add the parsley, lemon juice, and ¼ cup of the reserved clam liquid. Again mix well. Salt and pepper to taste.

Wash the clam shells and separate the tops and bottoms. Fill the shells with the prepared mixture, then dust the tops with the hot paprika. Place the stuffed shells on a cookie sheet and bake for 10 minutes.

You can place these little treasures on a platter and garnish with kale, which is rather like seaweed, or put fresh seaweed on the platter and serve them that way.

moshup mussels

SALLY LASKER

What makes this dish especially good is gathering the mussels yourself. We try to go musseling at least once a year, usually in the early spring when we need a good reason to get outside and take a long walk on the beach. SERVES 12 TO 15

4 to 5 dozen small mussels
2 cups white wine
$\frac{1}{2}$ cup chopped tomatoes
$\frac{1}{2}$ cup chopped shallots
$\frac{3}{4}$ cup coarsely chopped cilantro
$\frac{1}{4}$ teaspoon hot sauce
$\frac{1}{2}$ cup heavy cream
4 tablespoons unsalted butter
Freshly ground black pepper
1 loaf crusty French bread

Scrub and debeard the mussels.

Combine the wine, tomatoes, shallots, $\frac{1}{2}$ cup cilantro, the hot sauce, and heavy cream in a large pot. Bring these ingredients to a boil. Cook and stir for 2 minutes. Add the mussels and turn the heat down to a simmer. Cover the pot and cook for 5 to 10 minutes, until all the mussels have opened. (I start peeking around 6 minutes.) Take the mussels out with a slotted spoon and transfer them to a serving bowl.

Simmer down the cooking liquid until it is reduced to 2 cups; this will take another 5 to 10 minutes. Add the butter, stirring your sauce gently. Turn off the heat and add black pepper to taste. Pour the sauce over the mussels, sprinkle with the remaining cilantro, and serve immediately. The sauce is so delicious you will want to sop it up with the French bread.

pears *on* dark bread

PATRICIA CLIGGOT

Pears on Dark Bread is a recipe that was passed along from one friend to another. It is easy, delicious, and looks pretty. It's important to me that food looks really good, tastes just as good, and doesn't necessarily take a lot of time. The combination of the sweet pear and sharp cheese is wonderful. We served this at our gallery opening, and it was a big hit. SERVES 15

4 ripe pears
1 tablespoon fresh lemon juice
2 teaspoons honey mustard
1 package miniloaf pumpernickel bread
1 pound Hunter's cheese or Monterey Jack
Large leafy greens and purple grapes, to decorate platter (optional)

Heat the oven to 400 degrees.

Rinse and peel the pears, then slice them thinly. Squeeze a little lemon juice on the sliced pears to prevent browning.

With a butter knife spread a thin layer of the honey mustard on each piece of pumpernickel bread. Lay out the slices of bread on a cookie sheet. Cover each one with a thin slice of cheese and lay a pear slice across the top. Heat in the oven for 5 minutes, until the cheese bubbles. These are best served warm. Garnish your serving tray with greens and purple grapes, if desired.

seared tuna *with* wasabi aioli *on* crispy wonton

ANNIE FOLEY

I arrived on the Vineyard in the midseventies on the last $25 DC10 flight out of La Guardia. We touched down on a misty night, and I was met with a bottle of Champagne and driven down seemingly endless dark roads to a warmly lit gathering, where much merriment ensued—and still does! The best part of living here remains walking on the beaches when no one else is around. SERVES 15 TO 20

½ cup vegetable oil, for frying
1 package fresh wontons
1 teaspoon kosher salt
½ pound best-quality sushi tuna
1 tablespoon wasabi powder
½ cup mayonnaise
¼ cup black sesame seeds

Heat the vegetable oil in a large frying pan to 360 degrees. It is important that it be hot enough.

Cut the wontons in quarters. Fry them until they are lightly browned, then use metal tongs to remove them. Place the fried wontons on paper towels. Clean the frying oil out of your frying pan.

Salt both sides of the tuna. With your frying pan heated to medium-high, sear the tuna on both sides. The tuna needs to be browned on both sides and rare in the middle, so cook approximately 30 seconds on each side.

Slice the tuna on the diagonal in about ¼-inch slices.

Mix the wasabi powder with the mayonnaise. It works very well to put the wasabi-mayonnaise in a plastic ketchup or mustard squeeze bottle.

Place a piece of tuna on a wonton crisp. Squeeze some aioli on top and sprinkle with sesame seeds. These are so delicious that your platter will be empty before you've set it down. They are best made just before serving so that the tuna is at its freshest.

WINTER
dinner

It's cold in January on the Vineyard, just the way we like it. (If it was warm weather we were after we'd be living on a different island, like Hawaii or St. Lucia.) Sometimes, if it's not cold enough, the ponds don't freeze and the ice skates don't make it up from the basement where they live the rest of the year, dusty, hanging from a nail. But when the thermometer hits that magic number, the water freezes, and the skates are retrieved.

Ice hockey on Parsonage Pond, figure skating on Duarts, ice boating on Squibnocket—these are just a few of our favorite winter pastimes. There are a few days when the lucky (and intrepid) ones might even be able to skate from Chilmark all the way to Aquinnah, seeing the island in a new light, from a new angle. Skating is our winter reward, something we can count on to liven up a cold snowy day.

After one such skating afternoon, we heard that Alexandra (Al) Styron and her fiancé, Ed Beason, were planning a visit to the Island, an event certain to liven up *any* kind of day. One tantalizing phone call from New York suggesting a weekend on the Vineyard was enough to set the wheels in motion.

I ran into Nina dropping the kids off at school. "Al and Ed are coming. Let's have a dinner party." "Great, I'll call Michael and Sydney." Once we pinned Al down for certain she offered her house, as long as she didn't have to cook.

Al, with her New York, off-island energy, gets away with hosting and not cooking because she adds new meaning to the phrase "the life of the party." And with her impending wedding to the equally fabulous Ed and her soon-to-be-published first novel, she was entitled to be the center of attention, not a worker bee. We agreed upon a sit-down dinner—and we had plenty of friends to choose from between year-rounders, weekenders, and off-islanders coming up to get their winter Vineyard fix.

Ben deForest, one of our favorite chefs on the island, offered to cook the main course, provided he could have early access to Al's kitchen. Nina decided on an appetizer, and Peter and Nancy, coming from Boston on a motorcycle, would bring something small enough to fit in their saddlebags, maybe olives. Sydney agreed on a side dish, and Annie chose dessert. Carly kept wavering between pasta and bread pudding. I would assemble a winter salad and Gary, naturally, would bring the dressing.

In the end, we would be twelve altogether at a table that seats ten. Always up for a challenge, I volunteered to try to figure out where to put everyone and make the table look gorgeous.

The day arrived and, with it, a phone call from Carly. "I've decided on bread pudding!" she said enthusiastically. "Oh, and Mike and Diane are here and I invited them to come, too. Diane's bringing her favorite cherry pie. Is that okay?" Mike and Diane, plus a homemade cherry pie, would be more than okay, all welcome additions to our dinner. But now we were fourteen. Determined to eat at the table, we scoured Al's basement for stools, chairs, nightstands—anything and everything we could find to sit on or eat off.

While Ben prepared two main courses—roasted leg of lamb and broiled codfish with saffroned island tomatoes—Nina and I foraged through Al's cupboards and closets, gathering up her grandmother's linens and china. Once we squeezed everything onto our makeshift table—the best linen, bouquets of deep red roses, and scattered seashells—it looked beautiful in the blue winter light, a real Vineyard still life.

The night was full of the intimacy and good cheer of close friends together, and Peter, who somehow managed to get his banjo from Boston to Chilmark on the back of his bike, serenaded us with classic banjo tunes over coffee and dessert. Tomorrow we might again brave the cold and check the ponds for skateable ice, but tonight we would be cozy and warm. Wally, Al's seven-year-old yellow Lab, found a place on the sofa, nestled under Diane's arm. Her blissful expression mirrored our own.

cheese snips

NINA BRAMHALL

The first time my mother made these, I popped one into my mouth thinking it was a cookie and gave my unsuspecting taste buds quite a shock. They are peppery and crumbly and do look more like dessert than an hors d'oeuvre, but it's the breakfast cereal in the lineup that gives them their special je ne sais quoi. SERVES 16

1 cup (2 sticks) unsalted butter, at room temperature
$^1/_2$ pound sharp white cheddar cheese, grated
2 cups all-purpose flour
2 cups Rice Krispies
$^1/_2$ teaspoon salt or to taste
1 tablespoon Tabasco sauce (less if you want them milder)
1 teaspoon cayenne pepper (less if you want them milder)

Heat the oven to 325 degrees.

Put the butter and cheese into a food processor and pulse until well combined. Add the flour and Rice Krispies and pulse again. When well blended add the salt, Tabasco, and cayenne.

Drop the dough by teaspoons onto an ungreased cookie sheet. If you want, you can leave them as is, or flatten them with your hand for smoother snips. Bake the snips for 15 minutes. Turn off the oven and leave them in for at least 2 hours and up to overnight. This crisps them up.

broiled codfish *and* saffroned tomatoes

BEN DEFOREST

SERVES 6

2 pounds fresh codfish
Salt and freshly ground black pepper
4 tablespoons unsalted butter, melted
4 tablespoons olive oil
2 carrots, finely chopped
2 stalks celery, finely chopped
1 red onion, finely chopped
4 shallots, finely chopped
1 tablespoon chopped garlic
1 tablespoon grated fresh ginger
6 tomatoes, coarsely chopped
1 bunch lemon thyme, half finely
    chopped
2 pinches saffron threads
1 cup dry white wine

Cut the cod into 6 portions. Season them with salt and pepper. Place the fish in a baking dish, brush with the melted butter, and set aside.

Heat the olive oil in a large saucepan over medium-low heat. Add the carrots, celery, onion, shallots, garlic, and ginger and cook for 10 minutes, until softened. Next add the tomatoes, chopped thyme, and saffron. Turn the heat up to medium and cook for another 5 to 7 minutes. Pour in the wine and cook until the liquid reduces to half the amount, 3 to 5 minutes. To this add 3 cups of water. Continue cooking to reduce the sauce by one third.

Broil the codfish for 10 to 15 minutes, until fish is tender and just beginning to flake. Transfer cod to a serving platter. Spoon sauce over and around the cod. Garnish with whole sprigs of lemon thyme and serve hot.

asparagus *and* salsify bundles

BEN DEFOREST

Salsify, or oyster plant, is an old-fashioned root vegetable making a comeback.

SERVES 6

  2 bunches asparagus (about 2 pounds), ends trimmed off
  2 pounds salsify, peeled and cut into thin spears
  2 bunches scallions, stems trimmed off
  2 tablespoons unsalted butter, melted
  Salt and freshly ground black pepper

Steam the asparagus spears in a steamer over about 2 inches of boiling water for 2 minutes, then shock the asparagus by submerging them in a bowl of ice water to arrest the cooking. Steam the salsify in the same manner, cooking for 5 minutes, then shock in ice water. Steam the scallions for 30 seconds.

Turn on the broiler.

To assemble the bundles, divide the asparagus and salsify into 6 bundles. Wrap each bundle with 2 or 3 steamed scallions and make a knot. Paint the bundles with melted butter. Place them on a baking sheet and broil for 4 minutes.

Remove to a serving platter. Season with salt and pepper to taste and serve hot.

winter pear sauté

BEN DEFOREST

This makes a delicious accompaniment to Asparagus and Salsify Bundles (see page 207). SERVES 6

3 Bosc pears
2 tablespoons olive oil
Salt and freshly ground black pepper
2 tablespoons unsalted butter
2 tablespoons brown sugar

Peel and core the pears, then slice into wedges. Put the pears and olive oil into a saucepan over medium heat and cook approximately 10 minutes. Season with salt and pepper. Add the butter and sugar. Cook just until the butter melts. Toss the pears gently to coat with sugar, remove from heat, and serve.

brown rice *with* tahini dressing

SYDNEY BACHMAN

My friend Carol taught me a version of this brown rice dish. She serves it hot over green salad. I also like to eat it cold for lunch over salad with a vinaigrette dressing. When I served this rice dish with roasted chicken on top to my boyfriend, he proposed to me. SERVES 6

the rice
  2 cups short-grain brown rice
  ½ cup wild rice
  1 medium onion, cut into ¼-inch slices
  2 tablespoons olive oil
  ¼ cup raw sunflower seeds
  ¼ cup raw pumpkin seeds
  1 tablespoon raw sesame seeds
  ½ cup yellow unsulphured raisins
  ¼ cup tamari (or soy sauce), diluted with ¼ cup water

the dressing
  2 tablespoons tahini (ground sesame paste)
  Juice of 1 lemon
  3 cloves garlic, finely chopped
  1 teaspoon salt
  ¾ to 1 cup olive oil

To make the rice, bring 4 cups of water to a boil in a large saucepan. Add the brown and wild rices and reduce heat. Cover and simmer until all of the water is absorbed (approximately 45 minutes). Sauté the onions in 1 tablepoon olive oil in a skillet until golden brown. Remove to a small bowl. Put the sunflower and pumpkin seeds in the same pan and cook over medium heat until browned, 3 to 5 minutes. Remove to the bowl with the onions. Repeat with the sesame seeds.

   Add 1 tablespoon olive oil to the pan and sauté the cooked rice for 1 minute, then fold in the onions, seeds, and raisins. Finish by adding the tamari and sauté 1 minute more.

   To make the dressing, put the tahini, lemon juice, garlic, and salt into a blender. Pulse until smooth. Slowly add the olive oil with the blender on low.

cherry pie

DIANE SAWYER

made by pam gentner

To me, cherry pie is both chaste and romantic. It says tell me your secrets, stay all day. MAKES ONE 9-INCH PIE

the filling
  2½ cups canned tart cherries
  1 cup cherry juice (tart)
  2½ tablespoons quick-cooking tapioca
  1 cup sugar
  ½ teaspoon ground cinnamon

the crust
  2 cups pastry flour
  1 teaspoon salt
  ⅔ cup very cold vegetable shortening, cut into small cubes
  ¼ to ½ cup ice water

  2 tablespoons milk
  1 tablespoon sugar

Heat the oven to 450 degrees.

To make the filling, pour the cherries and cherry juice into a large bowl. Add the tapioca, sugar, and cinnamon. Mix the ingredients until they are well blended. Let the mixture stand for 15 minutes.

To make the piecrust, put the flour, salt, and shortening into a food processor and blend, pulsing, until the mixture resembles coarse crumbs. Slowly add ¼ cup ice water.

Pulse to mix in the water, just until the dough is moist and begins to form a ball. If the dough seems too dry add a little more ice water.

Turn the dough out onto a lightly floured cutting board. Handling it as little as possible, form it into a ball, then divide the ball in half. (If you're not used to working with pastry, chill it.) Roll out one half into a 12-inch round and gently press into a 9-inch pie tin. Trim off any excess dough to ½ inch beyond the rim. Pour the cherry filling into the crust. Roll out the other half of the dough into a 12-inch round. Cut the dough into ten ½-inch strips.

Lay five strips across the filling, spacing them evenly. Lay the remaining strips on top at a right angle to the first strips, again spacing them evenly. Trim off the excess lattice ends, fold the rim of the shell up and over the lattice strips, and crimp. Brush the top with milk and sprinkle with sugar. Bake for 10 minutes, then reduce the heat to 350 degrees and bake an additional 40 to 45 minutes, until the filling is bubbly and the crust is golden.

winter wellington
bread and butter pudding

CARLY SIMON

Of all the Dukes I have known in my time, Wellington was the only one willing to divulge to me his secrets on the subject of bread and butter pudding. Not the Duke of Earl, the Duke of Ellington, or the Duke of Snider. Only Wesley. Dear Wesley. And here is what he said (as he was putting on his boots, sipping sherry, and orchestrating Napoleon's downfall). He said, "My dear, custard is the way to greatness. It is the bread and butter of life, that which unites the common people with the real chickens." I always wondered what he meant by the chicken thing, but I assume it referenced the eggs in the custard. He said, "Make a bread and butter pudding for your next potluck dinner on the Vineyard, and I shall come and unite the Tories. There are many hidden Tories in the town of Tisbury, and if you make it, I shall come." Because I had my feverish eye on his boots, I listened carefully and long as he grew further intoxicated by the very mention of the rich ingredients and finally passed out in a self-induced trance. Getting out of England with the recipe was not easy, as the border guards look for big, big secrets of this luscious sort. The boots went by the guards with no problem at all, and I wear them now as I write this. SERVES 12 TO 16

½ cup raisins (I like golden; or if you like candied fruit, use that instead)
½ cup liqueur (kirsch or Kahlúa)
½ cup (1 stick) unsalted butter, softened
1 loaf of day-old French bread (not sourdough), cut into 12 slices (no ends)
2½ cups milk
2 cups light cream
1 cup granulated sugar
2 teaspoons vanilla extract
4 large eggs
5 egg yolks
Handful of confectioners' sugar

Heat the oven to 350 degrees. Butter a 9×13-inch baking dish.

Soak the raisins in the liqueur in a small bowl for 20 minutes. Generously butter both sides of the bread slices.

Put the milk, cream, granulated sugar, and vanilla in a saucepan over medium heat and heat until hot, but do not boil.

Beat the eggs and egg yolks together in a large bowl.

Spread the plumped-up raisins and liqueur over the bottom of the pan. Place the buttered bread slices in a single layer over the raisins.

Pour the hot milk and cream into the egg mixture, stirring while pouring. Pour this mixture through a strainer over the bread. Place the baking dish in a larger pan with an inch of water in it. Place this double tray into the oven for 50 to 55 minutes, until a knife poked into the center comes out clean. Remove from the oven. Turn on the broiler.

Sprinkle the Wellington with confectioners' sugar and place under the broiler until the sugar browns.

Serve hot or warm.

VALENTINE'S
dessert
PARTY

I firmly believe that to give is far better than to receive. Love is the ultimate gift, and on Valentine's Day one can never give too much. Red hearts, the symbol of the day and expression of love, begin to show up in store windows as early as the third week of January. By February, red hearts appear everywhere: in your cereal, on your chocolate, your paper towels, cookie cutters, jewelry, ice cube trays—even heart-shaped red ravioli finds its way onto the supermarket shelves.

The origin of this symbol can be traced back to 10,000 B.C. Some artistic soul painted a red heart on a woolly mammoth on a cave wall in Spain; this is believed to be the oldest rendering of the image of the heart. Today, this symbol means, among other things, that Valentine's Day is rapidly approaching.

Long ago, on the eve of St. Valentine's Day, people drew lots to determine their sweethearts and potential marriage partners, a custom lasting well into the eighteenth century. Most of us, now capable of picking our own sweethearts, enjoy the extra attention associated with Valentine's Day.

Romance and food have long gone hand in hand. A home-cooked dinner for two with a little extra emphasis on candles, flowers, and dessert can help shake the winter blues. A visit to a favorite restaurant with an excellent bottle of wine and a baby-sitter who is willing to stay late can truly put things in perspective.

Celebrating Valentine's Day before or after February 14, in the company of good friends, can turn a gray winter week into a love fest. This February, I decided to do just that.

Midnight Farm, my store and home away from home, was a perfect location for a Valentine's potluck dessert party. For one thing, it has far more couches and square footage than home. The sound system is superior and if you look out the window into the night, you might catch the glow of the ferry coming into the harbor.

Decorated with shimmering tea lights and vases of flowers in various shades of hot pinks and reds, the store was infused with a romantic energy all its own. Then came the desserts. Friends, dressed elegantly, walked in with tantalizing plates of sweet artistic expression: baklava, cappuccino dips, carrot cake, French love horns, fruit croustade with brandy sauce, Jigg's favorite lemon meringue pie, linzer tart, praline cheesecake, Spanish flan, and chocolate-hazelnut fortune cookies, to name just *some* of the mouthwatering desserts that covered every inch of two seven-foot tables.

The socializing took place around the food, with the exception of a few folks who strayed to the other side of the store. Early spring arrivals of shoes, sweaters, and bags turned out to be as much of a temptation as the strawberries dipped in chocolate.

Looking around the room I realized I have this eclectic group of friends, some of whom I've known since childhood and some I've only just recently met. Our common thread is an incredible passion for this extraordinary island and community. There was such an abundance of love and laughter in the room on that February night, I shall always remember the potluck at Midnight Farm.

cappuccino dips

CATHERINE URBAN

An incredibly sophisticated and delicious cookie! MAKES 4 DOZEN

1 cup (2 sticks) unsalted butter, softened
⅓ cup granulated sugar
½ cup brown sugar, packed
1 tablespoon instant coffee dissolved in 1 teaspoon hot water
2 ounces unsweetened chocolate, melted
1 large egg
2 cups all-purpose flour
1 teaspoon ground cinnamon

the glaze
1 cup semisweet chocolate chips
4 tablespoons unsalted butter

Combine the butter and sugars in a large mixing bowl and beat with an electric mixer until light. Add the dissolved coffee, unsweetened chocolate, and egg. Beat well. Stir in the flour and cinnamon. Cover with plastic wrap and refrigerate for at least 1 hour.

Remove from the refrigerator and divide the dough in half. Shape each half into a log (it helps to flour your hands a bit) approximately 1½ inches in diameter. Roll logs in waxed paper and chill several hours or overnight.

Heat the oven to 325 degrees.

Slice logs into ¼-inch slices. Place on an ungreased cookie sheet. Bake for 8 to 10 minutes. Let cool for a minute or two before removing from the sheet to a cooling rack.

To make the glaze, melt the semisweet chips and butter in a bowl set over simmering water or in a microwave. Remove from heat and stir until smooth. Dip half of each cookie in the glaze. Place on waxed paper to set.

french love horns

MARGOT DATZ

My daughter Scarlet and I had a mirthful afternoon concocting these little love trumpets. They call for patience, as does love itself. The lovely thing about these trifles is that they can be popped right into your mouth, a great finger-food dessert. We can attest to this—we popped about ten into our mouths before all was said and done. MAKES ABOUT 2 DOZEN

1 cup all-purpose flour, sifted
1 cup finely chopped nuts
¼ cup unsalted butter
¼ cup vegetable shortening
⅔ cup light corn syrup
⅔ cup brown sugar, packed
1 ounce semisweet chocolate
2 egg whites
2 bunches fresh mint
½ cup plus 3 tablespoons granulated sugar
1½ cups heavy cream
3 tablespoons liqueur (amaretto, Grand Marnier, or some other favorite)
24 fresh raspberries

Heat the oven to 325 degrees and grease a cookie sheet.

Combine the flour and nuts in a large bowl. Melt the butter and shortening in a saucepan. Add the corn syrup and brown sugar and bring to a boil. Remove from heat. Gradually pour and mix into the flour-nut mixture. Drop by teaspoons (not too full) onto the cookie sheet, about 3 inches apart. Bake for 8 to 10 minutes. Cool 1 minute (they will harden more as they cool). Remove carefully and roll at once to form a cone. (If they begin to harden set back in the oven for a couple of minutes to soften again.) Repeat with the remaining batter.

Let the cones cool on a plate. Melt the chocolate in a microwave or over simmering water. Paint (with a pastry brush) the inside rim and tip of the cones with melted chocolate. Let cool. You now have your horns.

Beat the egg whites until frothy in a medium bowl with an electric mixer. Brush 24 to 30 mint leaves with egg whites. Drop these coated leaves into a plastic bag with ½ cup of granulated sugar. Shake until the leaves are coated with sugar. Carefully remove them from the bag and lay them out on a rack to set.

Whip the cream in a large mixing bowl with electric beaters. Beat until almost stiff, then add 3 tablespoons granulated sugar and the liqueur and whip until stiff. Spoon stiff cream into a pastry bag fitted with a star tip. Pipe cream into the cones, swirling at the top. When the cones are filled, garnish each with a fresh raspberry and a mint leaf, to resemble a rosebud.

sandy's superb carrot cake

SANDY CICIORA

Sandy Ciciora started coming to the Vineyard in the 1970s, working as a summer waitress at the famous Homeport restaurant in Menemsha. She moved to the Island full-time in the mid-1980s and subsequently married a native. With her came all her recipes, a favorite among them being her ever-popular carrot cake. It's the perfect dessert for potluck gatherings any time of the year. Everyone loves it and it's usually one of the first desserts consumed. Sandy is a nurse in the maternity department at the Martha's Vineyard Hospital and the mother of twins, so her spare time is at a premium. One of her favorite activities is spontaneous potluck dinners with Island friends, and this recipe is a must-serve. MAKES ONE 9-INCH LAYER CAKE

the cake
1¼ cups corn oil
2 cups granulated sugar
2 cups plus 2 tablespoons flour
2 teaspoons baking powder
1 teaspoon baking soda
1 teaspoon salt
2 teaspoons ground cinnamon
4 large eggs
4 cups grated carrots
1 cup raisins
1 cup flaked sweetened coconut
1 cup chopped walnuts

the frosting
3 ounces cream cheese, softened
½ cup (1 stick) softened butter
1 teaspoon vanilla extract
2½ cups confectioners' sugar

Heat the oven to 350 degrees. Butter and flour two 9-inch round cake pans.

To make the cake, combine the oil and granulated sugar in a large mixing bowl. Stir well. Sift the flour, baking powder, baking soda, salt, and cinnamon into a separate bowl.

Mix half of the dry ingredients into the oil and sugar mixture. Add the eggs one at a time, alternating with the remainder of the dry ingredients. Stir well after each addition. Add the carrots, raisins, coconut, and nuts. Mix well. Pour batter into the cake pans and bake for 50 minutes, until a cake tester comes out clean. Cool on racks.

To make the frosting, mix the softened cream cheese and butter until smooth. Beat in the vanilla. Gradually add in the confectioners' sugar a little at a time until smooth and creamy. Frost the cakes generously.

enlightened chocolate cake

ALICE BERLOW

If gravity is the force that attracts bodies toward the center of the Earth, then chocolate is the force that attracts bodies toward one another. SERVES 10 TO 12

10 ounces bittersweet chocolate, chopped
1 cup (2 sticks) unsalted butter, cut into pieces
5 large eggs
1$^{1}/_{4}$ cups granulated sugar
5 tablespoons all-purpose flour
1$^{1}/_{2}$ teaspoons baking powder
$^{1}/_{4}$ teaspoon ground cinnamon
Confectioners' sugar, for serving

Heat the oven to 325 degrees; butter and flour a 10-inch springform pan.

Combine the chocolate and butter in a heavy-bottomed saucepan and place over low heat. Watch carefully and stir often until the mixture is melted and completely smooth. Remove from the heat.

Beat the eggs and granulated sugar together in a large bowl until well blended. Sift the flour, baking powder, and cinnamon together over the eggs and fold in. Gradually fold in the chocolate mixture. Scrape the batter into the pan.

Bake the cake for 20 minutes, then cover the pan with foil and bake for another 25 to 30 minutes. Remove the foil and stick a cake tester in the center; the tester should have some moist crumbs attached. Cool the cake completely on a rack.

Run a knife around the edge of the cake, then release the sides of the pan. Transfer to a cake plate and sift confectioners' sugar over the top.

linzer tart

MARIAN EMERY

brought by randa emery blair

Although there are many linzer tart recipes out there, my mother, Marian, has come up with this one after twenty years of baking. This dessert is great year-round, but I associate it most closely with winter. A few weeks before Christmas the baking starts, and my mother's kitchen is transformed into what appears to be a linzer tart factory. My father and I silently hope she bought extra chocolate, as we break off pieces from the stacks of bars on the counter when we pass through the kitchen. She makes tarts to give to relatives and friends—the list of recipients grows each year—and to bring to holiday parties. Part of the anticipation of Christmas for those close to my mother includes waiting for her homemade tarts. Is it the raspberry, the hazelnuts, or the chocolate that makes it so divine? You decide.

MAKES ONE 9-INCH TART OR TWO 7-INCH TARTS

3 ounces bittersweet or semisweet chocolate, chopped
¾ cup sugar
1 cup whole almonds or toasted hazelnuts
1½ cups all-purpose flour
½ teaspoon ground cinnamon
Pinch of salt
9 tablespoons cold unsalted butter, cut into small pieces
1 large egg
1½ tablespoons fresh lemon juice
1 cup raspberry jam
Confectioners' sugar, for dusting

Heat the oven to 350 degrees. Line the bottom of a 9-inch (or two 7-inch) removable-bottom tart pan with parchment paper.

Combine the chocolate, sugar, and nuts in a food processor. Pulse until finely ground. Add the flour, cinnamon, and salt. Continue pulsing to combine. Add the butter and pulse until mixture becomes crumbly. Transfer to a large mixing bowl.

Beat the egg and lemon juice together in a small bowl. Pour this slowly into the flour mixture, stirring (I use a fork) until ingredients come together. Remove 1 cup of the dough. Roll it between 2 sheets of waxed paper to about ⅛-inch thickness. Place this in the freezer for 5 minutes.

Remove enough of the remaining dough to make a ½-inch-thick rope that will fit the diameter of the pan. Press the rest of the dough from the bowl into the bottom of the tart pan. Now press the dough rope onto the sides of the pan to create the crust edge. Spread the raspberry jam across the bottom of the tart with the back of a spoon.

Remove the dough from the freezer and discard the paper. Cut the dough into 1-inch strips. Use strips of dough to create a lattice across the top of the tart. Or, use a 3-inch cookie cutter to cut out shapes for the top of the tart.

Bake for 50 minutes for a 9-inch tart or 35 to 40 minutes for 7-inch tarts.

Remove the tart from the oven and let it cool on a rack. Push up on the bottom of the tart to remove it from the pan sides. Dust with confectioners' sugar and serve.

fruit croustade
with brandy sauce

NATALIE CONROY

For entertainment during the long cold Island winters, a small group of foodies get together for intimate dinner parties. Among the guests are usually one or two Island chefs so I try to treat them to something special. This simple and spectacular dessert is a favorite. SERVES 20

> 4 pounds dried fruit (prunes, apricots, figs, your choice)
> 2 cups granulated sugar
> 1 cup brandy
> 1 pound (4 sticks) unsalted butter
> 30 sheets of phyllo dough (you'll need 2 boxes), defrosted
> Confectioners' sugar, for dusting

Combine the dried fruit, 1½ cups sugar, 2 cups water, and the brandy in a large bowl. Stir to dissolve the sugar. Cover and refrigerate overnight. Remove the fruit from the refrigerator and drain the syrup into a small saucepan. Roughly chop the fruit and set aside. Slowly reduce the syrup by half over medium-high heat. Reserve this sauce.

Set an oven rack in the upper third of the oven and heat the oven to 400 degrees.

Cut a piece of parchment paper to fit the bottom of a 10½ by 15-inch sheet pan. Melt the butter in a medium saucepan. Paint the paper and sides of the pan with butter. Cut 18 sheets of phyllo dough to 10½ by 15 inches. Cover with a damp towel. Cover the remaining 12 sheets with a damp towel as well. Lay a sheet of cut phyllo over the parchment paper, brush phyllo with butter, and sprinkle with a heaping teaspoon of sugar. Lay the second sheet over the first and repeat with butter and sugar. Repeat with the third layer, then bake for 5 minutes (some ovens may take longer), until nicely browned. Remove from the oven, brush with butter, and repeat with 3 more layers of phyllo, butter, and sugar. Brown these 3 layers. Remove from the oven, brush with butter, and repeat with 3 more layers of phyllo, butter, and sugar—you'll now have 9. Spread the soaked fruit evenly over the 9 layers of phyllo.

Now begin the process again: 3 sheets buttered, sugared, and browned, repeating until you have 9 layers on top of the fruit as well.

Next form the top of the croustade. Scrunch up the 12 pieces of uncooked phyllo dough to make rough piles and arrange these on the top of the baked layers. Drizzle with remaining butter, sprinkle with sugar, and brown for several minutes. (You can turn heat up to broil and place sheet under broiler, watching carefully.) Let cool for 20 minutes. Drizzle the reserved syrup over all and dust with confectioners' sugar.

Transfer carefully (I use 2 spatulas) to a large serving platter. Cut portions with a sharp knife. Serve on dessert plates. Any extra sauce can be spooned around the croustade.

chocolate-hazelnut
fortune cookies

JOSEPH AND REBECCA NORRIS

These chocolate-hazelnut fortune cookies are as much fun to make as they are delicious to eat. Guests can't wait to open their personal fortune or "love quote." They are the hit of every party.

For the fortunes, cut ¹/₄-inch strips of paper (I used red for Valentine's Day). Using a silver or gold pen, write love quotations (our local librarian downloaded great lists of them off the Internet). MAKES 18 COOKIES

4 large egg whites
1 cup superfine sugar
¾ cup all-purpose flour
¼ cup cocoa powder
Pinch of salt
¼ cup unsalted butter, melted
3 tablespoons heavy cream
1 teaspoon vanilla extract
2 tablespoons hazelnut oil (available in gourmet and specialty markets)

Heat the oven to 400 degrees.

Whip the egg whites in a mixing bowl with an electric mixer on medium speed. Add the sugar, increase speed, and mix until smooth. Place the flour, cocoa, and salt into a sifter. Sift into the egg-sugar batter. Continue to mix until well combined. Next add the butter, heavy cream, vanilla extract, and hazelnut oil. Mix again until combined.

Spray a cookie sheet with nonstick spray. (I use a nonstick baking mat.) Spoon 1 tablespoon of the batter in 3 places on the cookie sheet (the two lower corners and the upper center). Spread gently with the back of the spoon into 5-inch circles. Bake until slightly crisp at the edges, but still pliable in the center, 6 to 8 minutes.

Remove from the oven. Immediately take cookie disks off the tray one at a time (so they stay pliable as you fold the first one). Quickly fold the disk in half, pinching about 2 inches of the top edges together to seal. Immediately take the open loops at each end with your thumb and forefinger of each hand and push inward to form the fortune cookie. Repeat with the next two disks. Then start another batch.

When all the cookies are cooled, slip in the fortunes. Many will have an easy opening, but for those that don't, fold the fortune tightly and stuff it in a corner of the cookie.

crème celeste *with* strawberry sauce

JAIME HAMLIN

This incredibly delicious and easy recipe was given to me by my dear friend, artist extraordinaire, Margot Datz. You can put it together in about 10 minutes, but start it in the morning so it has all day to set. I've put it into star-shaped molds for Christmas and heart molds for Valentine's Day and surrounded it with pureed frozen strawberries, caramelized rhubarb, raspberries, or blackberries. SERVES 6

2 cups heavy cream
1¼ cups sugar
1 tablespoon unflavored gelatin
2 cups plain yogurt
1 (10-ounce) package frozen strawberries, thawed
fresh raspberries for garnish

Combine the cream and 1 cup sugar in a saucepan over medium heat. Stir to dissolve the sugar and cook until bubbles form at the edge. Sprinkle the gelatin over ¼ cup water in a small saucepan. Heat over low heat until the gelatin dissolves. Stir into the cream and sugar mixture. Whisk in the yogurt. Pour into a mold. Chill until set (overnight is best).

Combine the thawed strawberries and ¼ cup sugar in a food processor or blender. Process until smooth. Unmold the crème celeste onto a serving platter. Pour sauce around it, strew with raspberries, and serve.

spanish flan

SALLY LASKER

This is a very elegant dessert that consistently gets raves and is easy to make. I call it "the Old Standby." My mother-in-law has been making this flan for more than forty years and it's one of those wonderful, timeless dishes that are always a hit.

SERVES 12 TO 16

- 1¾ cups sugar
- 3 large eggs
- 5 egg yolks
- 2 cans evaporated milk
- 2 teaspoons vanilla extract
- 2 cups fresh fruit (strawberries, blackberries, raspberries, kiwi, peaches, or any combination), for garnish
- 1 tablespoon Grand Marnier (or other orange liqueur)

Heat the oven to 350 degrees. Fill a large bowl with ice water.

Combine 1 cup sugar and ½ cup water in a 2-quart flan pan (heavy pudding pan) over medium-high heat. Boil this mixture; do not stir, just swirl pan around. Cook until the caramel turns a deep amber color. Remove from the heat and set the pan in a bowl of ice water to arrest cooking. Move pan around so the caramel coats the sides of the pan as well. Keep in water until it's hard and starts to crack. Set aside.

Combine the eggs, egg yolks, ¾ cup sugar, evaporated milk, and vanilla in a large mixing bowl. Whisk until well combined. Pour through a strainer into the flan pan. Cover tightly with foil. Place the flan pan into another pan filled halfway with hot water. Place in the oven and cook 1¼ hours, or until firm. Remove from the oven. Let cool on a rack for 20 minutes. Refrigerate overnight.

Remove the flan from the refrigerator. Unmold onto a large serving platter— one that will allow at least a 2-inch border. Place fresh fruit around and on top of the flan. Heat the Grand Marnier in a small pan until warm, then drizzle it over the flan. Serve at once.

piecrust

2½ cups all-purpose flour, plus extra for dusting
1 teaspoon salt
2 tablespoons sugar
12 tablespoons (1½ sticks) unsalted butter, cut into small pieces and well chilled
8 tablespoons solid vegetable shortening, well chilled
6 to 8 tablespoons ice water

Mix the flour, salt, and sugar together in a large bowl.

Add the butter and use a pastry cutter (or your hands) to cut the butter into the flour until it resembles coarse cornmeal. Be patient, it takes a while. Still working the dough mixture, cut in the shortening. Continue until the butter and shortening bits are no larger than small peas, and the dough holds together when a small bit is pressed between your fingers.

Add the ice water gradually, tossing it in with a fork.

Turn the pie dough onto a floured work surface, and fold it over itself a few times. (Don't fold too much.) The dough will be soft but will firm in the refrigerator. Divide in two, and wrap each disk in plastic wrap.

Refrigerate at least 1 hour before using and up to 2 days. If you are making only one pie, freeze the other half of the pastry.

To roll the crust, dust your work surface with 1 tablespoon flour and sprinkle another tablespoon on top of the dough. Apply light pressure while rolling from the center out. Roll across the entire surface evenly. Lift and turn the dough each time you roll it to keep it from sticking and to keep the shape round.

Transfer the dough to a pie tin by gently folding the dough in quarters, centering it in the pan and unfolding it. Do not stretch the dough. Gently work the dough into the pan, lifting it to get a smooth fit along the bottom and up the sides. Trim the edges to within ½ inch of the lip of your pie plate. Tuck the overhanging dough back under itself so the folded edge extends ¼ inch beyond the pan lip. Press firmly to seal.

For a decorative edge the simplest thing to do is press the fork tines against the dough, flattening it against the rim of the pie plate. You can also crimp the edges against the thumb and index finger of your other hand, creating scallops every 1 to 2 inches around the rim.

acknowledgments

This book, like any successful potluck event, would not have materialized with-out the help of many wonderful and talented friends. Carly Simon, you take the words "fairy godmother" to a new level. Your constant support, generosity, and over-the-top enthusiasm is amazing. Nina Bramhall, you met the challenge and went beyond. Your photographs captured the spirit, and your friendship is invalu-able. Patrie Grace, how many recipes did you finally make, bake, test, taste? You rule in the kitchen. To the potluck hosts: Allen and Lynne, Carly, Peter and Cora, Francesca and James, Nina and Paul, Al and Ed, thank you for inviting us into your homes. To all the potluck guests who brought such beautifully prepared, fresh, and delicious food, thank you. Louise Sweet and Carole Chapman, your flowers are gorgeous. To my staff at Midnight Farm—Jill Amado, Kate Shanor, and Heather Talkington—you make coming to work each morning a total joy. Randa Blair, thank you. John and Judy Hannon, Ron and Amy Guttman, there would be no store without you. Marian Young, you are a terrific agent and a great new friend. Roy Finamore and the staff at Clarkson Potter—what a team! You shared this vision; your editing skills are impeccable. Kate Suval, your potlucks are always the best. To the farmers and fishermen of Martha's Vineyard, thanks for bringing us the freshest food. To my parents, Cora and Peter Weiss, thank you for showing me the way. And finally, to my husband, Gary Stuber, and sons, Jules and Noah, bless you!

Raspberry Tart from *The Barefoot Contessa Cookbook* by Ina Garten, copyright © 1999 by Ina Garten. Used by permission of Clarkson Potter/Publishers, a division of Random House, Inc.

index

conversion chart
EQUIVALENT IMPERIAL AND METRIC MEASUREMENTS

American cooks use standard containers, the 8-ounce cup and a tablespoon that takes exactly 16 level fillings to fill that cup level. Measuring by cup makes it very difficult to give weight equivalents, as a cup of densely packed butter will weigh considerably more than a cup of flour. The easiest way therefore to deal with cup measurements in recipes is to take the amount by volume rather than by weight. Thus the equation reads:

1 cup = 240 ml = 8 fl. oz.   ½ cup = 120 ml = 4 fl. oz.

It is possible to buy a set of American cup measures in major stores around the world.

In the States, butter is often measured in sticks. One stick is the equivalent of 8 tablespoons. One tablespoon of butter is the equivalent to ½ ounce/15 grams.

LIQUID MEASURES

Fluid Ounces	U.S.	Imperial	Milliliters
	1 teaspoon	1 teaspoon	5
¼	2 teaspoons	1 dessertspoon	10
½	1 tablespoon	1 tablespoon	14
1	2 tablespoons	2 tablespoons	28
2	¼ cup	4 tablespoons	56
4	½ cup		110
5		¼ pint or 1 gill	140
6	¾ cup		170
8	1 cup		225
9			250, ¼ liter
10	1¼ cups	½ pint	280
12	1½ cups		340
15		¾ pint	420
16	2 cups		450
18	2¼ cups		500, ½ liter
20	2½ cups	1 pint	560
24	3 cups		675
25		1¼ pints	700
27	3½ cups		750
30	3¾ cups	1½ pints	840
32	4 cups or 1 quart		900
35		1¾ pints	980
36	4½ cups		1000, 1 liter
40	5 cups	2 pints or 1 quart	1120

SOLID MEASURES

U.S. and Imperial Measures		Metric Measures	
Ounces	Pounds	Grams	Kilos
1		28	
2		56	
3½		100	
4	¼	112	
5		140	
6		168	
8	½	225	
9		250	¼
12	¾	340	
16	1	450	
18		500	½
20	1¼	560	
24	1½	675	
27		750	¾
28	1¾	780	
32	2	900	
36	2¼	1000	1
40	2½	1100	
48	3	1350	
54		1500	1½

OVEN TEMPERATURE EQUIVALENTS

Fahrenheit	Celsius	Gas Mark	Description
225	110	¼	Cool
250	130	½	
275	140	1	Very Slow
300	150	2	
325	170	3	Slow
350	180	4	Moderate
375	190	5	
400	200	6	Moderately Hot
425	220	7	Fairly Hot
450	230	8	Hot
475	240	9	Very Hot
500	250	10	Extremely Hot

Any broiling recipes can be used with the grill of the oven, but beware of high-temperature grills.

EQUIVALENTS FOR INGREDIENTS

all-purpose flour–plain flour
coarse salt–kitchen salt
cornstarch–cornflour
eggplant–aubergine

half and half–12% fat milk
heavy cream–double cream
light cream–single cream
lima beans–broad beans

scallion–spring onion
unbleached flour–strong, white flour
zest–rind
zucchini–courgettes or marrow